7

NEW ECONOMIC DYNAMO

NEW ECONOMIC DYNAMO

Structures and Investment Opportunities in the Malaysian Economy

-independence
-NEP
-politics

FONG CHAN ONN
Faculty of Economics and Administration
University of Malaya

ALLEN & UNWIN
Sydney London Boston

First published in 1986
Allen & Unwin Australia Pty Ltd
8 Napier Street, North Sydney, NSW 2060 Australia

Allen & Unwin New Zealand Limited
60 Cambridge Terrace, Wellington New Zealand

George Allen & Unwin (Publishers) Ltd
18 Park Lane, Hemel Hempstead, Herts HP2 4TE England

Allen & Unwin Inc.
8 Winchester Place, Winchester, Mass 01890 USA

National Library of Australia
Cataloguing-in-Publication

Fong, Chan Onn.
New economic dynamo.

Includes index.
ISBN 0 86861 802 0 (pbk.).

1. Malaysia — Economic conditions. 2. Malaysia—
Industries. I. Title.

330.9595'05

Library of Congress Catalog Card Number: 85-73190

Set in 10/11 pt Times

Typeset and printed in Singapore by
Singapore National Printers (Pte) Limited

Contents

Tables

Figures

Abbreviations

ACCA	Association of Certified Chartered Accountants
ASEAN	Association of Southeast Asian Nations
ASN	Amanah Saham Nasional (National Trustee Shares)
BSE	Bumiputra Stock Exchange
CGC	Credit Guarantee Corporation
CPI	Consumer Price Index
CUEPACS	Congress of Unions of Employees in the Public and Civil Service
FELCRA	Federal Land Consolidation and Rehabilitation Authority
FELDA	Federal Land Development Authority
FTZ	Free Trade Zone
GDP	Gross Domestic Product
GGS	General Guarantee Scheme
GNP	Gross National Product
ICCH	International Commodities Clearing House
ISD	International Subscriber Dialing
ITM	Mara Institute of Technology
KKGP	Kongress Kesatuan Guru-guru dalam Perkhidmatan Pelajaran (Congress of Unions of Teachers in the Educational Service)
KLCCH	Kuala Lumpur Commodities Clearing House
KLCE	Kuala Lumpur Commodity Exchange
KLSE	Kuala Lumpur Stock Exchange
kwh	kilowatt hour
LCCI	London Chamber of Commerce Institute
LNG	Liquefied Natural Gas
MARA	Majlis Amanah Rakyat (People's Trustee Council)
MAS	Malaysian Airline System
MCA	Malayan Chinese Association
MECIB	Malaysia Export Credit Insurance Berhad

MIC	Malayan Indians Association
MIDA	Malaysian Industrial Development Authority
MIDF	Malaysian Industrial Development Finance Berhad
MISC	Malaysian International Shipping Corporation
MOIC	Malaysian Overseas Investment Corporation
MSA	Malayan Stockbrokers Association
MSE	Malayan Stock Exchange
MTUC	Malaysian Trade Unions Congress
Mw	Megawatts
NEB	National Electricity Board
NEP	New Economic Policy
NIC	Newly Industrialised Country
NITTCB	National Industrial Training and Trade Certification Board
NSB	National Saving Bank
OECD	Open Economics Corporation and Development
PERNAS	Perbadanan Nasional (National Corporation)
Petronas	National Petroleum Development Corporation
PVC	Polyvinyl Chloride
SEDC	State Economics Development Corporation
SEMS	Stock Exchange of Malaysia and Singapore
SES	Stock Exchange of Singapore
SLS	Special Loan Scheme
STD	Subscriber Trunk Dialing
TAR	Tunku Abdul Rahman College
UDA	Urban Development Authority
UKM	Universiti Kebangsaan Malaysia (National University of Malaysia)
UM	Universiti Malaya (University of Malaya)
UPM	Universiti Pertanian Malaysia (Agriculture University of Malaysia)
USM	Universiti Sains Malaysia (Science University of Malaysia)
UTM	Universiti Teknologi Malaysia (University of Technology of Malaysia)
UUM	Universiti Utara Malaysia (Northern University of Malaysia)

Preface

The twenty-first century is generally regarded as the 'Age of the Far East' because of the importance and potentiality of this region in the world economy. It is projected to be the fastest growing region over the coming two decades by many development economists. The Association of Southeast Asian Nations (ASEAN) represents a major group in this particular region. Malaysia, located in the heart of ASEAN, symbolises the youthful vitality of the grouping. From a per capita gross domestic product (GDP) of $US380 in 1970, it has grown to a per capita GDP of $US2,167 in 1984—making it one of the highest per capita GDP countries in Asia.

Notwithstanding the rapid economic growth Malaysia had enjoyed since the 1970s, it still remained generally an 'unknown' entity in the world economic scene. This is due principally to the fact that the country is one of the world's very few politically stable developing nations, and thus has not been a source of worldwide anxiety and focus. Further, it has also been living under the shadows of the super-economy of Japan and hyper-fast growth economies of Korea, Taiwan, Singapore and Hong Kong. This notwithstanding, the hard economic reality is that Malaysia since the 1970s has achieved an economic growth rate in excess of 7.7 per cent, making it one of the fastest growing economies in Asia. Malaysia is the world's largest exporter of natural rubber, crude palm oil, tin and a major producer of tropical hardwood, petroleum and natural gas. Further, by 1980, she has also emerged as a significant exporter of manufactured goods—being the world's largest exporter of electronic integrated circuits and components.

In such a rapidly growing nation with a diversified agricultural sector and a rapidly growing manufacturing sector, there exist ample investment opportunities for both the domestic and the foreign investors. The theme of this book is to highlight the full potential of this youthful nation; by describing and delineating its economic structures and its business and industrial environments, and then evaluating the opportunities that exist therein for investors, within the context of the New Economic Policy of the government. Readers, particularly potential investors, will find it useful to have a clear and concise picture of the Malaysian socio-political and economic environments, its infrastructural system, its financial environment, its manpower profile and marketing practices, as well as the extensive investment opportunities that are available to entrepreneurs, both foreign and domestic.

The vision of the nation is to attain the status of an advanced Newly Industrialised Country (NIC) by 1990. In order to achieve this, bold steps have been undertaken by the government to further diversify the agricultural and industrial sectors of the country. In the top tier of the strategy to achieve this economic vision comes the energy development programme which aims at extracting the vast reserves of oil and natural gas in off the east coast of Peninsular Malaysia, Sabah and Sarawak. In the second tier is the proposed petrochemical project in Trengganu, which seeks to produce upstream petrochemical raw materials using natural gas as feedstocks. Next comes other heavy industries such as the Trengganu integrated steel mill, the Labuan sponge iron plant and the made-in-Malaysia car. It is hoped that with the establishment of these heavy industries, sufficient demand could be generated to encourage more light and medium ancillary units to be established, producing components and parts for both the domestic and world markets. Finally in the fifth tier, with the successful establishment of these ancillary units, a whole range of industrial activities based on wood, palm oil and rubber could be developed to further deepen the Malaysian economy.

The bold strategy, then, could lead to the creation of a thriving manufacturing sector based on locally produced raw materials, and producing both light and heavy industrial goods competitively for the world markets. Given its vast natural resources, its ambitious industrial goal implemented within the context of an efficient and open economy, Malaysia has a more than even chance of achieving its vision of being an advanced NIC by 1990. It can, thus, be truly labelled as the new economic dynamo of the Far East region.

Acknowledgements

A research effort of this nature could not have been undertaken without the assistance and cooperation of many individuals and organisations.

I am particularly grateful to the many industrialists and business executives, whom I and my assistants interviewed in the context of my research for this manuscript. I am also grateful to many of the officers in the government departments, in particular the Malaysian Industrial Development Authority, the Economic Planning Unit, the Ministry of Finance, the Ministry of Trade and Industry for allowing me to extract some needed data from their files.

A special word of appreciation should be extended to the many research assistants who have been involved in this project. They include Foo Yuen Po, Sally Ho, Irene Low, Ng Wai Hong, Ng Suew Kiat, Khor Youk Lin. Their dedication to see the project over three years is much appreciated. The manuscript also benefited greatly from the prefeasibility studies conducted by the Master of Business Administration (MBA) class of 1984/85 on new investment opportunities in Malaysia.

We are also greatly indebted to the Vice-Chancellor, University of Malaya, Royal Professor Ungku Aziz for instilling the university with an environment of intellectual inquiry. It is only within this kind of environment that this manuscript could have been written.

Last, but not least, I thank my wife, Lay Hwa, and children Sian, Yi and Luien, for their inspiration and understanding in the course of the writing of this book.

Figure 1.1 Map of Malaysia

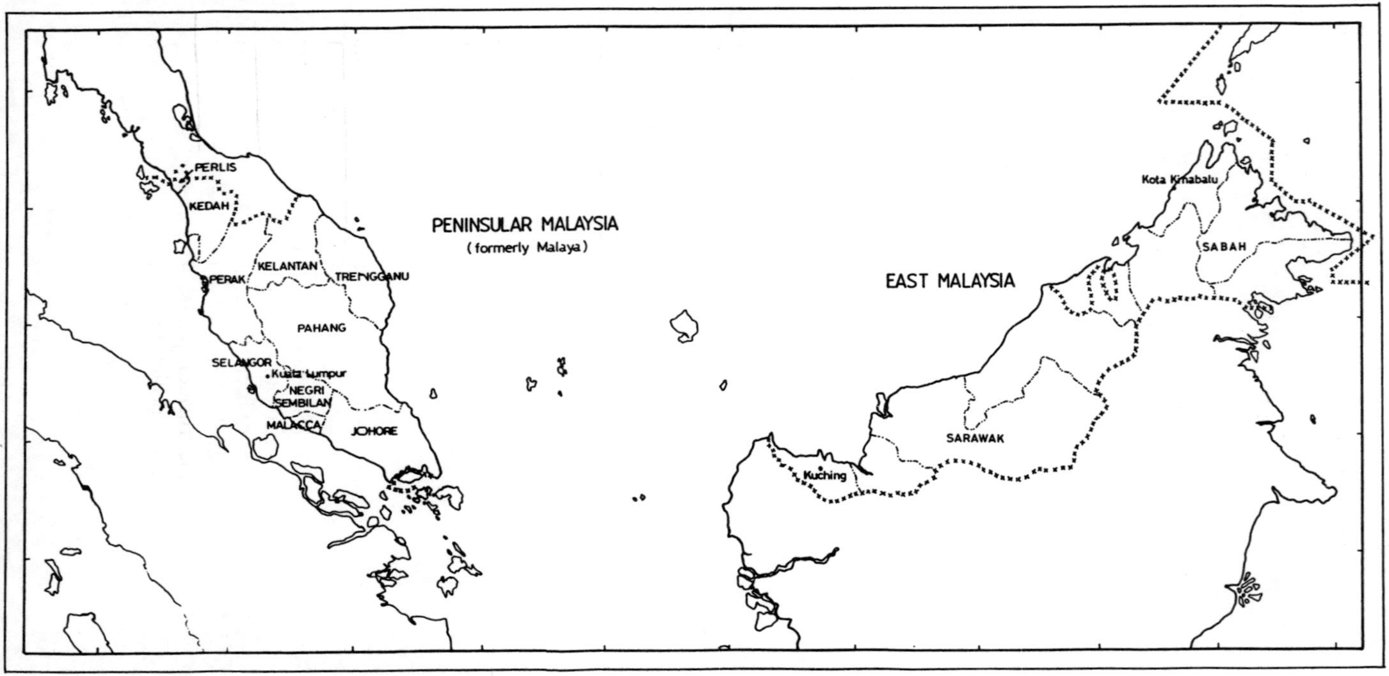

1

Socio-political environment

Malaysia covers an area of about 336 700 square kilometres (sq. km) occupying the Malay Peninsula and the states of Sabah and Sarawak in the north-western part of the Borneo Island. It is bounded by the Indian Ocean on one side and the South China Sea on the other. The country consists of eleven states, the Federal Territory of Kuala Lumpur in Peninsular Malaysia (formerly known as Malaya), and the two Borneo states of Sabah and Sarawak and the Federal Territory of Labuan. Peninsular Malaysia, covering 134 680 sq. km, is bounded in the north by Thailand and the south by Singapore while Sabah and Sarawak, totalling 202 020 sq. km lies to the north of Indonesia's Kalimantan (see figure 1.1).

The modern history of Malaysia began in the late eighteenth century with the colonisation of the Malay Peninsula by the British, through the 'founding' of modern Penang, by Sir Francis Light, in 1786 and the formation of the Straits Settlements (consisting of Penang, Malacca and Singapore) in 1826. By the early twentieth century, the whole of the Malay Peninsula, Sabah and Sarawak were completely under British control.

Organised economic development took place with colonisation. The British introduced rubber planting and large-scale tin-mining into the country in the late nineteenth century. As such activities grew, the British encouraged large-scale immigration of Chinese and Indians, to meet the labour needs of the tin and rubber industries. This resulted in modern Malaysia being a multi-racial country: the Chinese settling down mainly in the urban areas and engaging in the tin-mining and service activities; the Malays in the rural areas and engaging in their traditional farming activities; while the Indians were employed mainly in the rubber plantations.

The liberal immigration policy was terminated in the 1940s, and since then population growth in Malaysia has been due mainly to natural births amongst the settled population.

Malaya obtained its independence on 31 August 1957. It practises parliamentary democracy and is governed by a government formed by the elected majority party. The king of the country (the Yang Dipertuan Agung) is a constitutional monarch. He is selected from amongst the various state rulers, to serve as Yang Dipertuan Agung for a period of five years. The prime minister is appointed by the king, acting at his discretion, but ensuring that the appointed person has the confidence of the Parliament. In 1963, Malaysia was formed with the Federation of Malaya, Singapore, Sabah and Sarawak. In 1965, however, Singapore left the Federation and became a independent country.

Malaysia's population in 1980 was estimated to be 14.2 m. with 11.8 m. in Peninsular Malaysia, 1.0 m. in Sabah and 1.4 m. in Sarawak. The Malays and other indigenous people constituted about 53.9 per cent of the population, the Chinese about 34.9 per cent and the Indians about 10.4 per cent. The population, on the whole, was estimated to be growing at a rate of 2.5 per cent annually. The 1983 gross national product (GNP) of the country was $M64 082 million (at market prices), giving it a per capita GNP of $M4 513.[1]

Founding of Malacca to independence

The establishment of a settlement at Malacca by the Sumatran prince, Parameswara, in about 1400, marked the beginning of recorded history in the Malay Peninsula.[2] In 1403, the Chinese Admiral Yin Ch'ing visited Malacca. Malacca's ruler, Parameswara, approached the Chinese to protect Malacca from Siamese attacks; in 1405, Malacca officially became a vassal state of China. As a result of Chinese protection, Parameswara and his successors were able to devote most of their time towards establishing Malacca as a thriving port.

Parameswara married the Princess of Pasai in 1414, embraced Islam, and changed his name to Megat Iskandar Shah. His conversion established Malacca as an Islamic state. However, it was only during the reign of the third ruler, Sultan Muzzafar Shah, that the Empire of Malacca was really established. In fact, he was the first ruler to use the title of Sultan, and Islam was spread to all the territories taken over by him. Malacca flourished as a centre for Islam and a trading port of international importance. Further, he also established a social hierarchy that would survive to the modern era—a royal aristocracy comprising the Sultan, his family, and his court, a class of local leaders comprising district chiefs and village headmen, and a peasant class.[3]

In 1511, during the rule of Sultan Mahmud Shah, the Portuguese took over Malacca, which by this time was the capital of a kingdom that controlled most of the Malay Peninsula and much of Sumatra.

The Portuguese came to the East with four motives: trade, power, religion and gold. In Malacca, they were apparently more interested in trade and the main effects of their conquest was the dispersal of the Malays to the other parts of the Peninsula. The same was true of the Dutch after they took control of Malacca in 1641; they were more interested in maintaining Malacca as a base for strategic and trade considerations, rather than dominating the natives or mobilising them to produce goods for the mother country, as was the case in Indonesia.

Similar motives could be attributed to the British. They were looking for a good port for their ships, plying from India to China; and in 1786 they found it in Penang, which was taken from the Sultan of Kedah in return for verbal promise of protection from Siamese attacks and a periodical payment of some 6 000 Spanish dollars a year to the Sultan of Kedah. Later, in 1819, Sir Stamford Raffles founded modern Singapore. In 1824, through the Anglo-Dutch Treaty Malacca was given to the British in exchange for Bencoolen in Sumatra. Thus Penang, Singapore and Malacca came under the British rule. They were subsequently constituted as the Straits Settlements.

During the 1850s, Chinese mining settlements expanded rapidly into the Malay Peninsula. Clan wars among the Chinese were very common, particularly in Perak. To restore peace and order the Sultan of Perak appealed to the British to intervene. The subsequent intervention marked the beginning of the extension of British influence inland from the Straits Settlements and a pattern of indirect rule was established. In 1895, the four Malay states of Perak, Selangor, Pahang and Negeri Sembilan formed themselves into the Federated Malay States. British Residents were appointed to these states to take charge of the administration, while the Sultans continued to be responsible for matters of custom, religion and land.

British advisers were also appointed to Kedah, Perlis, Kelantan and Trengganu in 1909 when the Siamese, by treaty, transferred these states to the British. Johore agreed to accept a British adviser in 1914. These five states then became to be known as the Unfederated Malay States; each with its own legislative, executive, and judiciary, though their British personnel were interchangeable. They remained outside the Federation until after the end of World War II. The British developed Malaya extensively, but mainly for tin and rubber. Large tracts of land were alienated to various British companies such as Sime Darby, Harrison and Crossfields and Dunlop (these remained as major corporations in Malaysia today) for mining or plantation purposes, and an extensive road and railway network was built to serve these activities.

In order to unite the two Straits Settlements of Malacca and Penang with the Malay States, the Malayan Union proposal was put forward by the British on 1 April 1946. Three provisions of this proposal particularly grated upon Malay sensibilities—the loss of identity by individual states, the loss of sovereignty over the Malay States by their hereditary rulers, and the offer of citizenship to non-Malays on fairly liberal terms. This led to the formation of the United Malays National Organisation (UMNO) to oppose the Union; and because of this opposition, the Malayan Union proposal was withdrawn and replaced by the Federation of Malaya proposal.

The Federation of Malaya, consisting of the nine Malay States, Malacca and Penang, was established on 1 February 1948. Among its chief features was the desire of the British Government to prepare the Federation for eventual self-government. An Executive Council was established, and this was presided over by the High Commissioner. This body was the forerunner of the Parliament and Cabinet that would govern the country after independence. In addition, each of the states have a Chief Executive (Mentri Besar or Chief Minister) and a State Secretary.

With the formation of the Federation of Malaya, a number of important enactments came into force. These include:

1 The provision that almost every Malay became a federal citizen.
2 Non-Malays were automatically eligible for citizenship if both their parents were born and had resided in the Federation for 15 years.
3 It was also possible for a person to apply for citizenship on the basis of the applicant's own local birth or residence.

There were also special provision to safeguard Malay rights. The federal government was to be headed by the High Commissioner, in the names of the Malay rulers jointly with the British Crown. They shared in the act of legislation, and resumed sovereignty of their respective states. There was also to be a Conference of Rulers which the High Commissioner had to consult on matters of importance.

The Federation concept was not accepted by the Malayan Communist Party (MCP) and, in 1948, it chose to go underground and ferment a revolution that it hoped would lead to independence and the formation of a communist state. An Emergency was declared in response to this, but it had only one lasting consequence; it led to the resettlement of the Chinese squatters in the areas into 'New Villages'. In addition, the Emergency pitted government forces against guerilla forces and supporters who were mostly Chinese, and the conflict threatened to slow down the progress towards communal integration and harmony. Nonetheless, the Emergency quickened the pace of political development because the British, in trying to turn national sentiments against the MCP, decided to hold elections for seats on local councils that were to acquire increased responsibility for local matters. The Malayan Chinese Association (MCA) and the Malayan

Indian Congress (MIC) were then formed by the Chinese and the Indians respectively. In the first federal elections held in July, 1955, UMNO, MCA and MIC combined to form the Alliance Party and swept into power by taking 51 of the 52 seats on the Legislative Council. Its leader, Tunku Abdul Rahman became the Chief Minister.

After the elections a constitutional conference was held in London to consider the proposal for the appointment of an independent commission to draw up a constitution for a fully self-governing and independent Federation of Malaya. On 5 August 1957, the Federation of Malaya Agreement was concluded and on 31 August 1957 the Federation of Malaya secured its independence from the British.

To secure independence for the British colonies of Sabah, Sarawak, Brunei and Singapore, a federation of Malaysia, consisting of the Federation of Malaya, Sabah, Sarawak, Brunei and Singapore was proposed by Tunku Abdul Rahman and Lee Kuan Yew, the-then Chief Minister of Singapore, in 1961. However, the formation of Malaysia was opposed by the Philippines and Indonesia. Opposition by the Philippines stemmed from the unresolved question of its 'claim' to sovereignty over Sabah, while the Indonesian hostility stemmed from ideological, economic and political factors. Notwithstanding this opposition, the Federation consisting of Malaya, Sabah, Sarawak and Singapore was established on 9 July 1963 with special provisions for the new states which were:

1 Sabah and Sarawak were given greater control over local affairs, mainly in the areas of immigration, education and civil service.
2 Singapore was given autonomy in matters relating to language and education, and was also permitted to retain a substantial share of the revenue it derived from trade.

Two years later, in August, 1965, Singapore left the Federation to become an independent republic.[4]

Constitution and the parliamentary system

The Constitution is supreme in Malaysia, and it creates a strong central government responsible for most matters relating to the running of the country. Parliament derives its powers from the Constitution, which stipulates legislative power for both the federal and the individual state governments. Examples of matters in the federal list are external affairs, defence, civil and criminal law, and the administration of justice and citizenship; while those under the state list include Muslim law, land, agriculture, forestry and local government. The Constitution also specifies which are the concurrent subjects which either the Parliament or a State Legislative Assembly may legislate, and examples of them are social welfare, scholarships, town and country planning.

Constitutional provisions were also specifically provided for citizenship which was automatic for all persons born in the country after independence; a subsequent constitutional amendment, however, limited citizenship to those with at least one parent who was a citizen. Malay (Bahasa Malaysia) was made the national language and Islam became the state religion; but the practice of other religions was to be freely permitted. In addition, the Constitution also safeguarded the special positions of the Malays, reserved in the public services, of places and scholarships at educational institutions; and of permits and licences to conduct certain types of trade and business, and the reservation of certain lands as Malay Reserved Land and these are not transferable to the non-Malays. The purpose of these privileges is to encourage broader participation by the Malays in the economy.

The Parliament of Malaysia is made of three components:

1 the Yang Dipertuan Agung
2 the Senate (Dewan Negara) and
3 the House of Representatives (Dewan Rakyat).

Before any Bill can become law, it must have been passed by the Dewan Rakyat and the Dewan Negara and have received the Royal Assent of the Yang Dipertuan Agung.

The executive authority granted to the Yang Dipertuan Agung, king of the nation, selected from among the various state rulers to serve as king for a period of five years by the Constitution include the following: (i) the appointment of the prime minister, (ii) the right to dissolve the Parliament, and (iii) the convening of a meeting of the Conference of Rulers concerning the privileges, position, honours and dignities of the rulers. He is also the Supreme Commander of the Armed Forces and the Head of the Islamic Religion of his home state, Malacca, Penang, Sarawak, Sabah and the Federal Territories of Kuala Lumpur and Labuan. The Yang Dipertuan Agung also has the power to grant pardons, reprieves, and respites in respect of offences which have been tried by court martial, and in respect of offences committed in the Federal Territory.

The Dewan Negara House is the Upper House of the Parliament. It consists of 68 elected and appointed members: 26 elected members (two members elected by each of the 13 state Legislative Assemblies) and the remaining 42 members appointed by the Yang Dipertuan Agung. Membership of the Senate is limited to citizens aged 30 years and above and the life of the Senate is not affected by the dissolution of the Dewan Rakyat. The term of service of a senator is three years.

The Senate elects one of the senators as President and another as Deputy President.

The Dewan Rakyat comprises of 154 elected members: 114 from Peninsular Malaysia, 16 from Sabah and the remaining 24 from Sarawak. Membership to the Dewan Rakyat is limited only to citizens aged 21 and above, and the life of the House automatically eclipses when Parliament is dissolved. The Dewan Rakyat is fully elective; but it can elect a non-member as its Speaker and the person so elected is regarded as an additional member of the House. The Dewan Rakyat is the principal law-making body; with the prime minister, who is a member of the House, to command the confidence of the House.

The Cabinet headed by the prime minister, is the supreme policy-making body in the country. It is made up of ministers, who must be members from either the Dewan Rakyat or the Dewan Negara and are appointed by the Yang Dipertuan Agung, on the advice of the prime minister.

Parliament (consisting of the Dewan Rakyat and the Dewan Negara) is summoned to meet by the Yang Dipertuan Agung. He cannot allow more than six months to elapse between the last sitting in one session and the first meeting in the next session. He may end a session of Parliament or dissolve Parliament. Parliament continues for five years from the date of its first meeting. At the end of five years it is automatically dissolved, but it may be dissolved sooner. Whenever Parliament is dissolved, a general election is held within 60 days in Peninsular Malaysia and 90 days in Sabah and Sarawak from the date of the dissolution. Parliament must be summoned to meet not later than 120 days from the date of the dissolution.

The states of Selangor, Perak, Perlis, Kedah, Trengganu, Kelantan, Johor, Pahang and Negeri Sembilan made up the nine Malay states of the country and each of these states has a hereditary ruler who reign for life. The rights of succession to the throne are governed by the customs of the states, embodied in the constitution of each state. The ruler of all these states is known as the Sultan with the exception of Perlis and Negeri Sembilan. In Perlis, the ruler is known as the Raja while he is known as the Yang Dipertuan Besar in Negeri Sembilan. In the states of Malacca, Penang, Sabah and Sarawak, the head of state is the governor. Each state governor is appointed by the Yang Dipertuan Agung for a period of four years.[5]

New Economic Policy

Prior to 1969, the philosophical basis of economic development in the country was growth; economic growth induced through public investment in infrastructure, agriculture and rural development and, to a limited extent, industrial development. Although this strategy did strengthen the economy considerably, particularly since independence in 1957, the racial riots of May 1969 demonstrated clearly that the strategy failed to deal adequately with the main social and economic imbalances which characterised the plural Malaysian socio-political economy. The economic policy and programmes that were geared solely towards accelerating economic growth could not meet with the needs of the poor and the imbalances that exist among the various racial groups. Realising these limitations, one of the approaches undertaken since 1969 was the evolvement of a socio-economic foundation that could provide a viable and equitable participation for all racial groups in the development process. Such a framework was enunciated in the New Economic Policy (NEP) in the Second Malaysia Plan (1971–75). Specifically the twin objectives of the NEP are:

> The first prong is to reduce and eventually eradicate poverty, by raising income levels and increasing opportunities for all Malaysians, irrespective of race. The second prong aims at accelerating the process of restructuring Malaysian society to correct economic imbalance, so as to reduce and eventually eliminate the identification of race with economic function.[6]

The policy thus committed the nation to eradicate poverty in the country irrespective of race and to accelerate the process of social restructuring so as to eliminate the identification of race with economic function. The policy also committed the nation to achieve these goals within the context of an expanding economy so that no particular group may experience any loss or feel any sense of deprivation. The new strategy of growth with equity and distribution called for a realignment of policies and programmes to ensure the continuation of economic growth, and the equitable distribution of the benefits of this growth to the poverty groups (such as the rubber smallholders and the fishermen) and to the disadvantaged racial groups, particularly the Malays.

The operational targets of the NEP are detailed in the Second Malaysia Plan as well as the Mid-Term Review to the Second Malaysian Plan[7] and include the following:

1 A long-term target of eradiction of poverty was set up. By 1990, the incidence of poverty is targeted to be reduced to 17 per cent from the 1970 poverty incidence rate of 49 per cent.
2 A long-term target for restructuring of corporate-equity ownership and industrial employment is also specified. By 1990, ownership in the corporate sector should consist of 30 per cent Bumiputra equity, 40 per cent other Malaysian and 30 per cent foreign, compared to the 1970 breakdown of 1.9 per cent for Bumiputras, 23.5 per cent other Malaysian and 60.7 foreign. The '30:40:30' target, however, is a global target, and it need not be applied at the level of every individual

enterprise. Further, industrial enterprises are also required to have a workforce that reflect the racial composition of the country.

It must be pointed that, notwithstanding the '30:40:30' target, in absolute terms, all the specified groups are envisaged to experience significant expansions of their corporate holdings over the period 1970–90. It will enable non-Bumiputra ownership of share capital to growth at a per annum rate of 12 per cent and to expand its 1990 equity nine times more than its 1970 level. The foreign sector's equity share will increase at an annual rate of 8 per cent, and by 1990 its equity should be five times more than its 1970 level.

To achieve the above objectives, the government has implemented numerous programmes for the eradication of poverty, particularly rural poverty. These programmes include the establishments of new land schemes for modern agriculture activities, the establishments of agencies for the consolidation and rehabilitation of smallholders, the acceleration of industrialisation, particularly rural industrialisation, as well as the encouragement of the flow of labour from the rural areas to the urban centres.

In order to achieve the corporate equity target, the government has implemented a number of investment incentives and guidelines for the establishment of new projects, particularly industrial projects. Industrial projects that satisfy certain criteria in terms of export orientation, product group, equity and employment structure are given generous incentives including tax holidays. However, industrial projects that depend substantially on the domestic market are required to be majority Malaysian-owned, and the industrial employment of all industrial enterprises should reflect the racial composition of the country. Further, all existing and new industrial enterprises are required to be issued with the licence under the Industrial Coordination Act 1975.[8]

Notwithstanding the above guidelines, the government has pledged that the NEP requirements are global guidelines, and would be implemented flexibly. The extent of Malaysian and foreign ownership in a particular individual project will depend on the merit of the case, and could be even 100 per cent foreign-owned. In this context, factors which have bearing on the structure of equity include the amount of investment, the level of technology utilised, the location of the plant, proportion of production exported and the benefits accruing to the domestic economy through the spin-off effects of the project. Further, flexibility can be provided in the form of a time-frame within which the company has to attain the stipulated equity and employment profiles. This would allow the company to operate in the initial period with equity and employment structures that are more favourable to the investor; with the understanding that the stipulated equity and employment structures would eventually be achieved over a prescribed time-frame.

2

Economic environment

The decade of the seventies and early eighties witnessed rapid economic growth and structural transformation in the Malaysian economy. The gross domestic product (GDP), after having grown at about 6.5 per cent per annum during the 1960s, recorded an annual growth rate of 7.7 per cent over the decade 1971–82. This resulted in a rise in per capita income and major structural changes in the economy; by 1982, Malaysia's per capita GDP of $US1 860.00 ranked among the highest in Asia, next only to Republic of Korea, Japan, Singapore and Hong Kong.[1] The implementation of the twin objectives of the NEP, in conjunction with major efforts to expand modern sector activities, particularly manufacturing, have been the major factors accounting for the rapid economic growth and structural changes.

The changing structure of Malaysia's economy can best be summarised by figures 2.1 and 2.2. In 1957, the agricultural sector contributed about 45.7 per cent of the total GDP, and about 61.3 per cent of the total employment. By 1980, its contribution has declined to 29.6 per cent of the total GDP and 42.3 per cent of the total employment. On the reverse, in 1957, manufacturing only contributed about 8 per cent of the GDP and 6.4 per cent of the employment. By 1980, these figures have increased to 19.1 per cent and 15.8 per cent respectively. Figures 2.1 and 2.2 also indicate clearly the increasing importance of the Tertiary Sector, including services and retailing, in the Malaysian economy by the early 1980s. The factors accounting for these structural changes will now be elaborated.

Structure of production

Rapid economic growth in Malaysia began in the second half of the nineteenth century when the British extended their control from the

Figure 2.1 Composition of Gross Domestic Product (GDP) (1947–90)

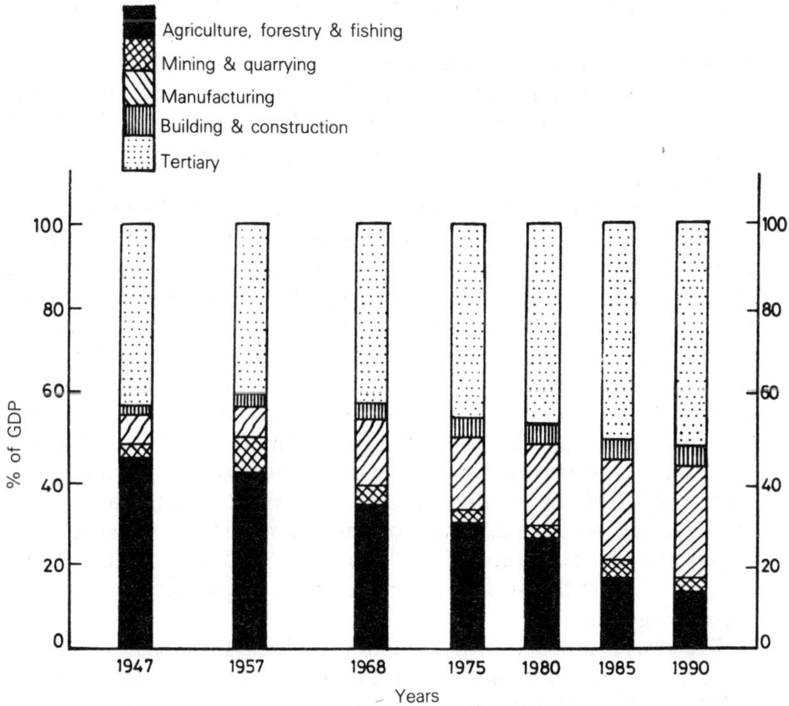

Figure 2.2 Composition of employment (1947–90)

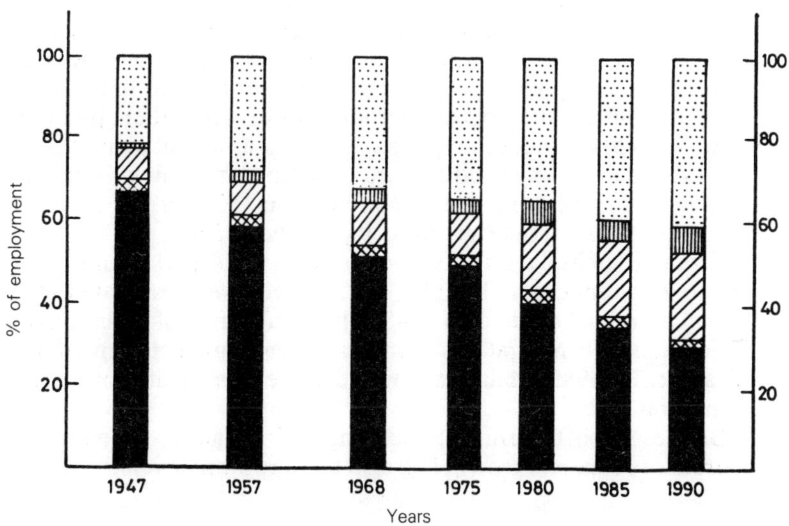

Straits Settlements to the Malay States. Rubber was introduced to Malaya at the end of the nineteenth century, and its rapid expansion in the early twentieth century was due to the development of the automobile industry in the West. At about the same time, the Industrial Revolution in the West led to a great demand for tin which was available in abundance in the Malay Peninsula. This led to extensive exploitation for the metal and by 1890, Malaya became the world's major producer of tin.

As a result Malaya had come to be almost wholly dependent upon rubber and tin for its export earnings by the early twentieth century. Hence any change in the world demand for these two commodities had an exaggerated effect on its economic performance. Realising this, since independence in 1957, the Malayan Government adopted an aggressive economic programme of diversification of the export earnings to include those based on palm oil, timber, petroleum, and manufactured goods. The measures adopted included policy measures (such as the 1959 Pioneer Promotion Act and the 1968 Investment Incentives Act) aimed at the promotion of industrialisation. The effects of this diversification in export earnings are summarised clearly in figure 2.3. In 1960, rubber was by far the single most important export earner of Malaysia. By 1980, its export receipts, though still significant, had been overtaken by petroleum and manufactured goods.

The emergence of petroleum and petroleum products as an important, if not the most important export earner for Malaysia by the early 1980s deserves some elaboration. Although hydro-carbon reserves have been explored in the country since the mid-nineteenth century it was only the increase in the crude oil price in 1973 that enabled Malaysia to commercially explore and extract crude oil from its off-shore fields. As a result of these exploration activities, by the mid-70s, Malaysia became a net exporter of petroleum and petroleum products. These surpluses in export earnings from the sector increased steadily and by the early 1980s, earnings from this sector have overtaken the export earnings from the other traditional sectors, such as rubber and palm oil, as well as manufactured goods. In 1980 Malaysia imported $1.9 m. of petroleum, mainly from Saudi Arabia and Singapore and exported about $6.7 m. of petroleum products, mainly crude oil from its off-shore field.

Estimates of Malaysia's reserves of Malaysia oil and natural gas are updated continuously. In 1982, the reserves were estimated at 2.3 billion barrels of crude oil and 48 trillion cubic feet of natural gas. A major liquefied natural gas plant has been constructed in Bintulu, Sarawak. By 1985, Malaysia would emerge as a significant exporter of natural gas.

Besides export earnings, the range of economic activities and sources of economic growth had also become more diversified. Other

Health Ministry also provides portable well water through community water supply schemes. Piped water supply is less feasible because the scattered nature of the rural population, makes it too expensive and does not allow for economies of scale, as the projects are necessarily small.

In Sabah and Sarawak, urban coverage of tap water increased from 95 per cent and 83 per cent in 1970 to 99 per cent and 93 per cent in 1980 respectively. Between 1981–85, about $M30 m. will be allocated to Sabah for pilot projects to be initiated under the National Rural Water Supply study, while Sarawak will receive $M20 m. With the accelerated implementation of rural supply programmes, the rural coverage is expected to reach 39 per cent in Sabah and 35 per cent in Sarawak by 1985.

Water rates are relatively cheap in Malaysia and are subsidised by the government. The public is currently paying between 77 cents and $M1.50 for every 4 500 litres while production costs vary between $M3 to $M5. The cost of water production is rising and is expected to shoot up to about $M11 for every 4 500 litres in future.

Sewerage

At the end of the 1970s, only the cities of Kuala Lumpur, Penang (George Town) and Kota Kinabalu had central sewerage systems. In 1970, 11 per cent of the urban population in Peninsular Malaysia was provided with central sewerage systems. In 1980, the population covered increased only to 14 per cent (half of whom were in Kuala Lumpur).

Over the period 1981–85, in order to improve health and sanitation standards, the sewerage programmes will continue to give emphasis to the replacement of inefficient and potentially hazardous methods of disposal with central water-borne sewerage systems, especially in heavily populated areas. A sum of $M200 m. was provided in the Fourth Malaysia Plan to implement these sewerage programmes.

Telecommunication facilities

In Malaysia, the system of telecommunication networks are mainly concentrated in the major urban areas in the more developed states of Peninsular Malaysia such as Selangor, Penang, Perak and Johore. Table 3.6 shows that the number of telephone subscribers increased from about 190 000 in 1976 to 490 000 in 1981, increasing the telephone-population ratio to 1.5 per 100 population in 1981. On the other hand, demand for telephones increased more than twofold from 260 000 in 1976 to 640 000 in 1981, resulting in a net increase of 10.4 per cent in the total number of telephone waiters in 1981.

Figure 2.3 Malaysia: major exports, 1960–80

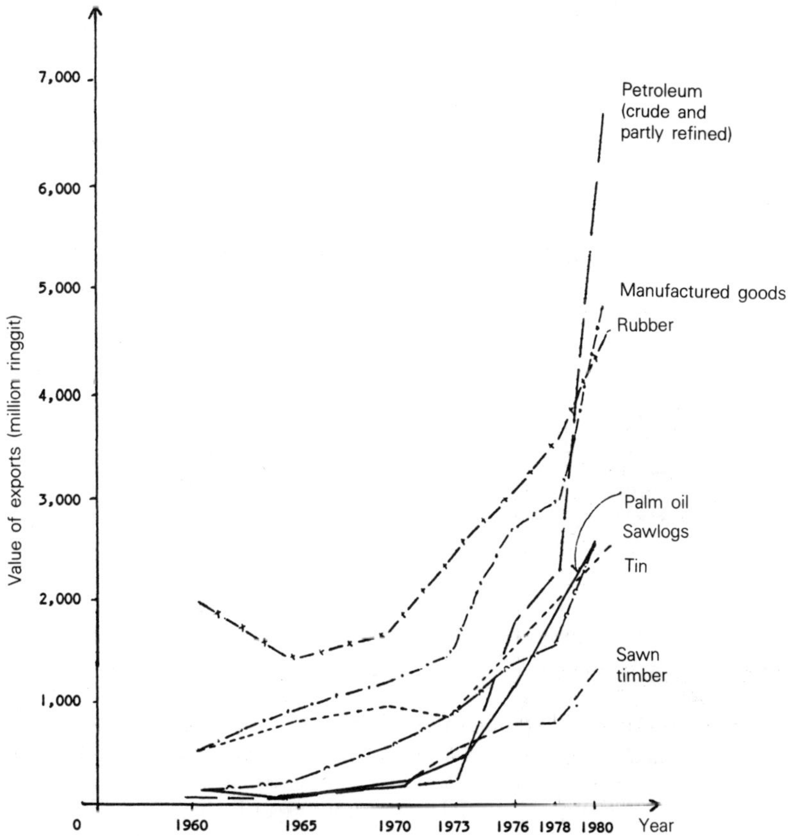

Source: Malaysia, *Bank Negara Quarterly Economic Bulletin, December 1981*, Bank Negara Malaysia, Kuala Lumpur, 1981.

structural changes included the change in the import pattern from a predominance of consumption goods in the 1960s to a predominance of intermediate and investment goods by the early 1980s. Further, there was an improved regional distribution of development, and a broader base for generating revenue for the financing of development. As a result of these developments, the GDP of Malaysia increased by over tenfold during the period 1960–80; from a GDP of $US2.29 billion in 1960 to a GDP of $US25.9 billion in 1982. Nevertheless, the Malaysian economy's annual growth rate of 7.8 per cent over the 1970s was slightly lower than the targeted rate of 8 per cent for the period.[2] The shortfall was due mainly to the low growth rate of the agricultural sector of only 4.3 per cent per annum. The manufacturing, construction, and services sectors recorded exceptionally high rates of percentage growth of 12.5, 9.6 and 8.6 per annum, respectively.

Sources of growth

As a result of the NEP, the 1970s saw a radical change in the role of the public sector in both industry and commerce. The government's participation in financing commercial and industrial enterprises had become significant; its role was not only one of creating a suitable environment for expansion of private enterprise, but also one of taking measures to stimulate and participate in private industries and commerce. Such measures include the revision of the Pioneer Industries legislation in the Investment Incentives Act of 1968, and the establishment of quasi-government corporations such as Perbadanan Nasional (PERNAS), Majlis Amanah Rakyat (MARA) and Urban Development Authority (UDA) to participate directly in commercial and industrial activities on behalf of the Bumiputras.[3] Other measures include the expansion of agencies empowered to invest government funds in trust for the Bumiputras in joint ventures with private enterprises. The direct participation of the public sector considerably expanded the Bumiputra's participation in the corporate wealth, and by 1990, it is targeted that the 30 per cent Bumiputra ownership of commerce and industry will be achieved. There has also been a continuation and expansion of direct government involvement in agriculture, through land settlement schemes operated by institutions such as Federal Land Consolidation and Rehabilitation Authority (FELCRA), Federal Land Development Authority (FELDA) and plantation schemes operated by the various State Economic Development Corporations.

In the early 1970s, the main source of growth for the economy was the domestic sector. During 1971–75, public sector development expenditure contributed significantly towards strengthening the overall domestic demand in the country, compensating for the reduced impact of exports and public investment. Over the period 1976–80, the growth of the Malaysian economy was also largely sustained by a strong expansion in aggregate domestic demand—in 1980 it rose by 24.4 per cent in nominal terms—and to a limited extent, accelerated external sector demand.

However, by 1982, with the continued uncertainty over the duration of the recession, a poor commodity-price situation, and high costs of international borrowings, the government was obliged to revise its budgetary expenditures, deferring projects of lower priority. As a result, public sector spending was expanded only mildly with a growth rate of 5.9 per cent, compared to a growth rate of 36.6 per cent in 1981. Further, after 1980, the external sector began to exert a contractionary impact on the growth of GNP. Exports of goods and non-factor services declined while imports of goods and non-factor services increased. This was largely the result of the fall in the volume and value of major export commodities such as rubber, tin, palm oil and to a lesser extent crude oil, the four products between them bring in more than 60 per cent of Malaysian foreign exchange and make up nearly a third of the country's GNP. Merchandise imports, on the other hand, continued to increase by 6.9 per cent in 1982, mainly due to strong demand for machinery, communication and transport equipment in the country to meet development needs.

Progress of industrialisation

As was elaborated previously, the major developmental strategy of the government since independence in 1957 has been the encouragement of industrialisation, initially on the basis of import-substitution and after 1968 on the basis of export-orientation. The rapid expansion of the industrial sector over the decade 1968–80 is vividly illustrated in figures 2.1 and 2.2. The share of manufacturing in GDP rose from 13.2 per cent in 1968 to 15.1 per cent in 1975. By 1980, the share of manufacturing in GDP was 19.1 per cent. On the reverse, the share of GDP contributed by the agricultural sector decreased from 35.0 per cent in 1968 to 31.1 per cent in 1975. By 1980, the agricultural sector's contribution to GDP was only 26.6 per cent. In absolute terms, over the period 1968–80, manufacturing's share in GDP tripled from $M1.1 billion to $M3.8 billion (giving it an annual growth rate of 10.9 per cent). Hence, over the decade, there was an absolute growth of about $M2.7 billion in the manufacturing sector's contribution to GDP. On the other hand, the absolute growth of the agricultural sector contribution to GDP for the period 1968–80 was only $M2.4 billion (that is an increase from $M2.9 billion in 1968 to $M5.3 billion in 1980).

In terms of employment, the performance of the manufacturing sector was also impressive. The share of employment contributed by the manufacturing sector increased from 9.1 per cent in 1968 to 15.8 per cent in 1980. The employment share of the agricultural sector, over the same time-frame, decreased from 51.6 per cent to 40.6 per cent. In absolute terms, the number of industrial jobs increased by approximately fourfold, from 215 000 jobs in 1968 to 805 000 jobs in 1980; an absolute increase of 590 000 new jobs. Over the same period, the absolute increase in agricultural employment was 848 000. Given the inherent higher labour productivity of industrial employment, the growth in industrial employment over the decade 1968–80 must be regarded as very impressive.

The detailed value added and employment profiles of the manufacturing sector over the period 1963–82 are shown in figures 2.4 and 2.5. From the figures, it can be seen that over this period, there was a marked structural change in the manufacturing sector. In 1963, in terms of value added, the major industrial groups were food manufacturing, rubber products (including processing off-estates), wood

Figure 2.4 Structure of value-added in manufacturing industries, Peninsular Malaysia

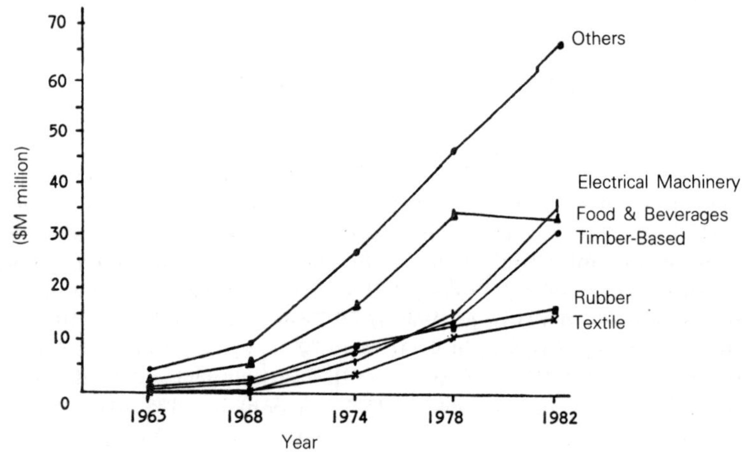

Figure 2.5 Employment pattern in manufacturing industries, Peninsular Malaysia

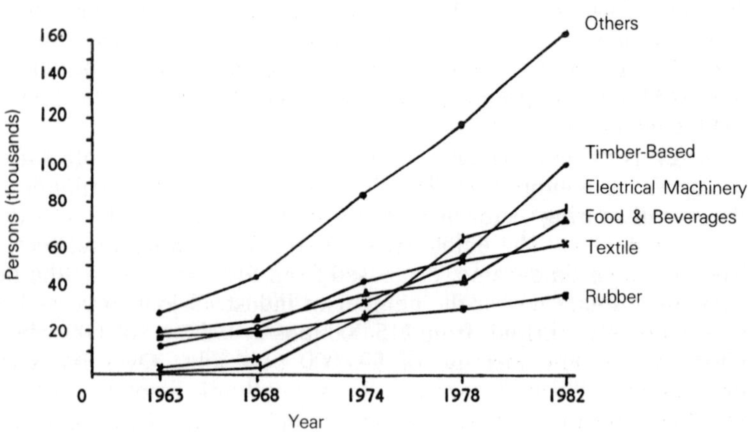

products, and beverages and tobacco. Food manufacturing contributed about 15.4 per cent of the industrial value added, while rubber products (including processing off-estates) contributed about 17.2 per cent of the industrial value added. The wood products and beverages and tobacco groups each contributed between 10 to 14 per cent of the industrial value added.

By 1974, because of the impact of the 1968 Industrial Incentive Act, a large number of new industries, particularly the export-oriented industries, were established. The major industrial subsectors in 1974 were food manufacturing, rubber products, wood products, and electrical machinery. Food manufacturing contributed about 17.3 per cent of the industrial value added, while each of the other four groups contributed between 9 to 13 per cent of the industrial value added. The emergence of electrical machinery, mainly in the form of electronics and electrical components, as a major industrial group in 1974, is an example of the growth of the export-oriented industries. The continued importance of food manufacturing (a large proportion of whose value added is exported), and textiles (mainly exported), also pointed to the growth of the export-oriented industries. On the reverse, domestic-oriented industries like chemical products, non-metallic products, and printing declined in their percentage contribution to the industrial value added between the period 1968–74.

By 1982, the effects of the growth of the export-oriented industries on the industrial structure were even more pronounced. There was a further significant increase in industrial value added of export-oriented groups such as food manufacturing, electrical machinery, timber-based products and textiles. Electrical machinery, by 1982, had increased its contribution to industrial value added to 22.8 per cent. The corresponding percentiles for the food manufacturing, timber-based product and rubber product were 15.7, 6.1 and 6.0 respectively. Textiles, a relatively minor group prior to the mid-1970s, had emerged as a major industrial group by 1982; with a contribution of about 6.4 per cent to the industrial value added. The growth of food, electrical machinery, and textile groups into major industrial groups, by 1982, indicated that the 1968 Investment Incentives Act was beginning to bear results. Most of the new firms, established for the production of electrical machinery (mainly electrical and electronics components) and textiles for exports were located in specially designed Free Trade Zones (FTZs).

The changes in the industrial employment profile paralleled the changes in the industrial value added. The main change, during the decade, in the industrial employment profile is the growing important role of the export-oriented industrial sectors in generating industrial employment. The electrical machinery (mainly electrical and electronics components) group's share of industrial employment increased dramatically, from only 1.7 per cent in 1968, to 15.6 per cent in 1982.

In fact, by 1982, in terms of industrial employment, the electrical machinery subsector had emerged to be the second largest group, next to the timber-based sector. Similarly, the textile subsector's employment contribution increased considerably, from 6.6 per cent in 1968 to 12.0 per cent in 1982.

However, food manufacturing (which is essentially an export-oriented industrial group), which saw its contribution to value added increased from 16.1 per cent in 1968 to 22.8 per cent in 1982, had its contribution to industrial employment reduced from 14.9 per cent in 1968 to 14.1 per cent in 1982. This may be attributed to the fact that, over the decade, there had been a steady upgrading of the food manufacturing technology utilised. By 1982, this had resulted in a more capital-intensive food manufacturing sector than that existing in the beginning of the 1970s.

The export performance of the manufacturing sector over the period 1970–80, is now analysed in greater detail so that the linkages between industrial structural changes and export performance can be highlighted. Table 2.1 presents the figures for the export of the major manufactured goods, which comprises food (and beverages and tobacco), textiles and footwear, wood products, manufacturing and transport equipment, and electronics and electrical components. The export of these major manufacturing goods accounted for 63.9 per cent of the total manufactured exports (or 15.3 per cent of the total gross exports) in 1970, and 82.5 per cent of the total manufactured exports (or 20.8 per cent of the total gross exports) in 1980.

Table 2.1 shows that the export of electronics and electrical components had increased from a value of $M31 million (or 6 per cent of exports of major manufactured goods) in 1970 to $M3 573 million (or 48 of major manufactured goods) in 1982. During the decade, the export of the electronics and electrical components industry grew at a phenomenal annual rate of about 57.7 per cent. This dramatic growth rate indicates both the success of the 1968 Investment Incentives Act in attracting electronics establishments, as well as the continuing strong international demand for these goods in the decade. The major items exported in this category include electronics microcircuits, transistors, diodes and conductor devices which were mainly exported to the USA and EEC countries.

Exports of textiles, which accounted for 8 per cent of the total major manufactured goods exports in 1970, also grew steadily at an annual rate of about 33.8 per cent per annum. By 1982, textile exports contributed about 11 per cent of the export of major manufactured goods, making it the second most important item of exports of the major manufactured goods.

Table 2.1 also indicates that the growth of export of manufactured goods was more rapid in the earlier part of the 1970s than the later part of the 1970s. For example, the annual growth rate of electronics

Table 2.1 Peninsular Malaysia: exports of major manufactured goods, 1970–82

Industry	1970		1975		1978		1980		1982		Average annual growth rate (%)	
	$Mm	%	$Mm	%	$Mm	%	$Mm	%	$Mm	%	1970–75	1975–82
Food, beverages and tobacco	84	(16)	232	(13)	289	(8)	475	(8)	533	(7)	22.6	11.2
Textiles and footwear	44	(8)	214	(12)	471	(13)	802	(13)	819	(11)	37.4	17.4
Wood products	20	(4)	197	(11)	362	(10)	467	(7)	413	(6)	58.1	10.0
Machinery and transport equipment	41	(8)	464	(26)	145	(4)	407	(5)	429	(6)	62.5	–1.1
Electronics and electrical components	31	(6)	411	(23)	1,702	(47)	2 832	(48)	3 573	(48)	67.4	26.6
Others	300	(58)	268	(15)	652	(18)	1 115	(19)	1 330	(22)	–2.2	23.1
Total exports of major manufactured goods	520	(100)	1 786	(100)	3 621	(100)	6 098	(100)	7 097	(100)	28.0	18.5
Total manufactured exports	814		2 873		4 179		6101		7 447			
Total gross exports	3 402		9 231		13 681		29 672		28 113			

Sources: Malaysia *Economic Report* Ministry of Finance, Kuala Lumpur, various years
Malaysia *Annual Statistics of External Trade* vol. I, 1970, 1975 and 1978, Kuala Lumpur: Department of Statistics

and electrical components exports for the period 1970–75 was 67.4 per cent. The corresponding annual growth rate in the period 1975–82 was 26.6 per cent. The difference in the performance, between the earlier and later part of the decade, was even more vividly indicated by the growth rates in the export of machinery and transport equipment. The export of this category of goods increased at an annual rate of 62.5 per cent during the earlier part of 1970s, but during the later part of the 1970s the corresponding rate was -1.1 per cent. The difference in export performance in the earlier and the later parts of the 1970s could be mainly attributed to the different economic conditions prevailing in the industrialised world over these periods. The GNP of the industrialised world, as exemplified by the OECD countries, grew at an annual rate of about 3.9 per cent in the period between 1970–75. The corresponding growth rate for the period between 1976–80 was only 2.4 per cent.

The slowdown in the export performance of the Malaysian industrial sector in the later part of the 1970s, as a result of the decline in the GNP growth rate of the industrialised world, is also clearly reflected in the number of new industrial projects approved or established in Peninsular Malaysia.

During the period 1971–75, a total of 2 119 projects were granted approval by the Ministry of Trade and Industry. Of these, 748 were given pioneer status, 130 investment tax credits, 54 labour utilisation relief and 73 other incentives, while the remaining 1 113 projects were approved without incentives. When in production, these projects involved a total called-up capital of $M2.8 billion and could provide employment to 294 000 people. The number of export-oriented projects approved (that is, those exporting at least 80 per cent of their output) increased from 33 in 1971 to 103 in 1975.

During the period 1976–80, of the 2 197 projects granted approval, 523 were given pioneer status, 330 were granted investment tax credits, 30 were granted labour utilisation relief and 63 were granted other incentives, while the remaining 1 078 projects were approved without incentive. Compared to the first part of the decade, there was a marked decrease in projects that were granted pioneer status. Further, all the new projects approved would generate employment to only 199 300 people, which was much less than the projected employment of the new establishments in the first part of the decade.

With respect to imports of manufactured goods, trade statistics available in Peninsular Malaysia indicated that the import value increased from $M2 764.2 m. to $M4 916.0 m. in 1982. On the other hand, the value of the export of manufactured goods in 1970 was $M813.6 m. (or 29.4 per cent of the value of total imports of manufactured goods); in 1982, the corresponding value in manufactured exports increased to $M7 447.0 m. (or about 151.5 per cent of the value of total imports of manufactured goods). This rapid increase in the ratio of the value of export of manufactured goods to import of manufactured goods indicates the steady deepening of the Malaysian industrial sector and reflects the success of the export-oriented industrialisation strategy.

Balance of payments

Over the period 1970–80, Malaysia enjoyed relatively healthy balance of payments on the current account, indicating that the economy was fairly resilient. The Malaysian balance of payments position for the period 1970–83 is as shown in figure 2.6. Over the decade of the 1970s and especially in the later half, Malaysia enjoyed consistent surpluses in the current account of the balance of payments, averaging about $M1.0 billion per year. These surpluses are partly attributed to the fact that by the later part of the 1970s, Malaysia had become a net exporter of crude oil. Notwithstanding this, there has been a significant increase in the deficits of the service account payment since the mid-70s, mainly due to increased payment on invisibles such as insurance, shipping, tourism and interest on borrowings.

By the early 1980s, the combined effects of the prolonged recession in the industrialised world together with a marked decline in the prices of primary commodities, and large interest payments on foreign borrowings, induced the country to suffer relatively major deficits in the balance of payments in the current account. In 1982, the deficits in the current account amounted to about $M6.0 billion. These large deficits in the current account indicate that even for a net exporting country like Malaysia, adverse effects would be induced if the prolonged recovery of the industrialised world does not materialise.

Price changes

The price levels and the cost of living in Malaysia remained remarkably stable by world standards during the 1960s. But the inflationary pressures began to emerge in the mid-70s. The rates of consumer price changes as measured by the consumer price index (CPI), which is also a proxy for a country's inflation rate for some ASEAN countries, USA and Japan are shown in figure 2.7

The world economy in the mid-70s was characterised by widespread and rapidly rising inflation, and low and negative rates of economic growth. Inflation reached its peak in 1974. Higher prices of food, oil and energy and other raw materials directly affected the severity of the inflation. During that year, consumer prices in the

Figure 2.6 Malaysia: balance of payments

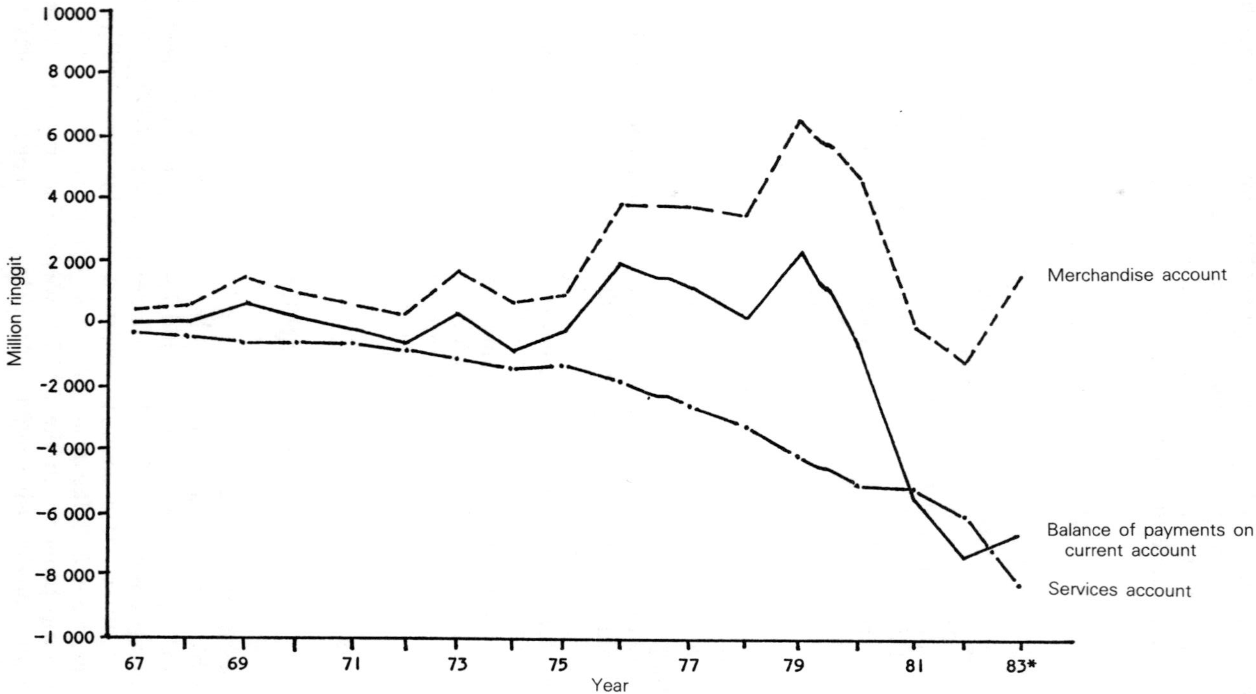

Source: Bank Negara Report, 1971–83
*estimated figures

Figure 2.7 Changes in consumer prices for ASEAN countries, USA and Japan

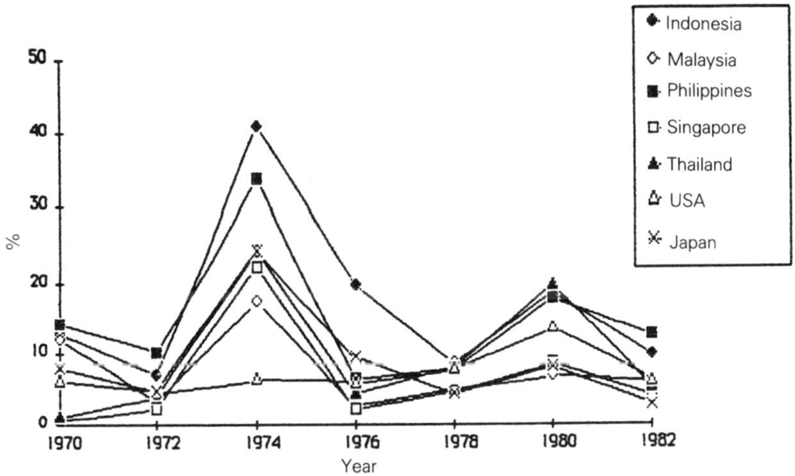

industrial countries of OECD increased by 13.3 per cent compared with an average of only 4.8 per cent in 1972. For ASEAN countries, the Indonesian consumer prices rose very rapidly in 1974, at an annual rate of 40.6 per cent; in Malaysia the consumer prices rose at an annual rate of about 17 per cent. This inflationary situation represented a sharp departure from a long period of price stability in Malaysia; in the 1960s, the rate of inflation averaged less than 1 per cent annually.

The rapid increase in the price levels over the period 1974–75 were generated mainly by the oil price increase of 1973; but the shortage of food supplies following crop failures in a number of major food-producing countries, further worsened the situation. This unfavourable world economic situation led to a build-up of inflationary pressures, resulting in sharp increases in the price of imports for Malaysia. This was further aggravated by supply constraints induced by hoarding, causing an unprecedented increase in domestic prices in 1973 and 1974, especially on items such as food, clothing and footwear, furniture, furnishings and household equipment. The price of residential and commercial buildings and industrial structures also increased substantially due to shortages of building materials and skilled labour, as well as speculative activities.

The rate of domestic inflation slowed down considerably from 1975 onwards—in 1975 the CPI rose by only 4.5 per cent—as a result of the improvements in the international inflationary situation and the success of anti-inflationary measures implemented by the government. These measures include a tightening of credit and the establishment of price controls on essential items such as rice, sugar and milk.

During the period 1976–80, the Malaysian CPI rose at an annual rate of only 4 per cent, comparatively much lower than any other ASEAN country. While the total CPI did not increase substantially, some sub-groups of the index, such as medical health expenses, rent, fuel and power, exhibited fairly high rates of increase.

The CPI began to show signs of an upward trend from 1980 onwards. For the years 1980 and 1982, the CPI rose at an annual rate of 13.7 per cent and 6.2 per cent, respectively. In 1982, a weaker domestic demand, slower rate of monetary expansion, and the overall easing of import prices kept the inflation situation under control.

Over the two year period of 1980–82, consumer prices for OECD countries declined more significantly in response to slower monetary policies pursued by these countries. The inflation rate in the OECD area eased to 7.8 per cent in 1982 from a figure of 12.9 per cent in 1980. The average rate of consumer price changes in ASEAN countries, following the OECD countries, had also decreased to about 6.2 per cent in 1982. The inflation rate in Malaysia was one of the lowest, at 5.8 per cent in 1982 and figure 2.7 shows consumer price changes in Malaysia since 1970, on the whole, were comparatively very low and stable.

Changes in employment

In line with the structural changes occurring in the economy there were significant changes in the sectoral employment pattern. Agriculture remains, however, by far the largest employer of labour, although the proportion of the total employment provided by agriculture fell from 50.5 per cent in 1970 to 40.6 per cent in 1980. However, manufacturing recorded the highest rate of employment growth of 7.6 per cent per annum in the decade 1971–80, while employment in construction and utilities also grew rapidly, at 6.8 per cent and 6.5 per cent per annum, respectively.

Total 1968 employment in Peninsular Malaysia was about 2.37 m. comprising 49.8 per cent Malays, 36.4 per cent Chinese and 13.8 per cent Indians and others. Within the primary sector the ethnic composition of employment was dominated by Malays, who formed 64 per cent of the employment in the sector. The Chinese and Indians constituted 23 per cent and 14 per cent respectively of the employment in the sector (see table 2.2). However, employment in the secondary sector consisting of mining, manufacturing, construction and commerce was dominated mainly by the Chinese, who formed 57 per cent of the sector's employment. Malays and Indians constituted

Table 2.2 Ethnic composition of sectors

Sector	% Composition		
	Malay	Chinese	Indians
Year 1968:			
Primary	63.5	22.6	13.9
Secondary	32.4	56.7	10.9
Tertiary	37.0	47.5	15.5
Year 1980:			
Primary	66.3	19.9	13.8
Secondary	39.8	51.1	9.1
Tertiary	47.0	41.6	11.4
Year 1990:			
Primary	59.0	29.4	11.6
Secondary	50.1	39.9	10.0
Tertiary	46.9	40.5	12.6

Source: N.S. Choudhry *Socio-Economic Sample Survey of Households-Malaysia, 1967–68: employment and unemployment* Kuala Lumpur: Department of Statistics, 1970
Malaysia *Fourth Malaysia Plan 1981–1985* Kuala Lumpur: Government Printer, 1981

32 per cent and 11 per cent respectively of the employment. The same trend was observed for the tertiary sector with the ethnic distribution being 48 per cent Chinese, 3 per cent Malays and 16 per cent Indians.

By 1975, after the implementation of the NEP, there were signs of improvement in the distribution of employment, although the changes were small. However, by 1980, the share of Malay employment in the tertiary sector increased to 47 per cent, the largest among the three ethnic groups in that sector. Further, the share of Malay employment in the secondary sector increased to 39.8 per cent. By 1990, it is projected that Malay employment in the secondary sector will increase to 50 per cent. Correspondingly, the share of the Chinese employment in the primary sector will increase from 19.9 per cent to 29.4 per cent and that of Indians will decline from 13 per cent to 10.8 per cent during the period.

Prospects for economic growth

Of all the factors that have enabled Malaysia to develop so rapidly over the past two decades, one of the most important is the availability of vast agricultural and mineral resources. Tables 2.3 and 2.4 summarise the vast natural resources that are still available in Malaysia. The availability of such extensive resources means that

Table 2.3 Availability of land in Malaysia, 1975

Category	Total area ('000 hectare)
Total land	32 792
Land under cultivation	6 075
Underdeveloped land suitable for cultivation	7 695
Land under forest	7 200
Tin mining areas	82
Others	11 740

Source: Young, K. et. al. *Malaysia: Growth and Equity in a Multiracial Society* Johns Hopkins University Press, Baltimore, 1980

Table 2.4 Reserves of natural resources in Malaysia

Category	Volume	
Crude oil (as at 1.1.82)	10 387.0	MBLS[1]
Natural gas: (as at 1.1.82)		
Non-Associated Gas	38.5	TCF[2]
Associated Gas	9.8	TCF
Forest	14.7	m. hectare

Source: Malaysia, Corporate Planning Department, Kuala Lumpur: Petronas, 1982
Malaysia *Timber Trade Review* 10, 4, Kuala Lumpur: Malaysian Timber Industry Board, 1981

Notes: [1]MBLS denotes million barrels
[2]TCF denotes thousand cubic feet

Malaysia possesses the revenue generating capacity required for further economic development. In 1982, Malaysia's gross capital formation amounted to 33.8 per cent of its GNP. This is the second highest amongst the Asian countries. Further, its debt service ratio was only 4.7 per cent of the value of merchandise exports in 1982. This is among the lowest in Asia, and implies that Malaysia still possesses extensive borrowing capacity required for its industrialisation programme. However, it must be pointed out that by 1983 Malaysia's external borrowing has reached a relatively high level of about $M30 billion. The availability of extensive natural resources and large capital generating (and borrowing) capacity, implies that with the necessary policy incentives and missionary zeal, even more ambitious development programmes, including high value added industries based on rubber, palm oil and natural gas could be successfully developed in the country.

In fact, the first step in industrial modernisation and technological upgrading has already been undertaken with the implementation of the Malaysia Car Project, the construction of the Trengganu petrochemical complex and the integrated steel mill, based on offshore natural gas as a fuel source. The technology utilised in these projects is among the best available, and with their successful completion, the first phase of the technological upgrading process would have been completed.

Another major factor that can lead to the achievement of more rapid economic growth is the stability of the Malaysian political environment. Since 1957, the country has experienced six general elections and four changes of prime ministers without loss of continuity in government policy and administrative machinery. The only black mark in the relatively stable political environment over the past two decades was the racial riots of 1969. The immediate post-1969 uncertainties were resolved and alleviated by strong governmental intervention, and the proclamation of the NEP. Since then, public confidence in the government has grown steadily, and by 1980, Malaysia stands as one of the most stable and democratic countries in Asia.

With the availability of extensive public sector revenue resources, the political leadership is now confident of the achievement of the 30 per cent Bumiputra target by 1990.[4] With this confidence in the government, and shifting its priority to promote growth and eradication of poverty, national unity in the coming decade could be further enhanced, thus enabling the country to attract the huge investments needed for industrial deepening.

Another important factor that will play a significant role in enabling Malaysia to achieve more rapid economic growth is the current international competitiveness of its labour-intensive industries, particularly the electronics industry. (Electronics will be the major growth industry of the next two decades.) Malaysia should capture on its current strength in this area (albeit in the assembling process), and encourage its current electronics establishments to upgrade their technology to that of wafer fabrication and mask-making. Indications are that some of the electronics plants are already proposing to fabricate wafers in their expansion programmes. An example of this is the proposed wafer production plant of Hitachi (Malaysia), which would shift the Malaysian electronics industry into the second stage of technology, prior to the acquisition of the first, and the most advanced level of circuit-design and mask-making. With more policy emphasis on upgrading the electronics industry, the chances for the country to emerge as a major producer of wafer and computer components by the end of the decade are excellent.

Having elaborated the positive factors, now the negative factors that may retard the achievement of more rapid economic growth must be expanded. Although it is generally felt that the 30 per cent Bumiputra corporate equity target could be achieved by 1990, the major part of this corporate equity would be held by public agencies in trust for the Bumiputra. In fact, according to the Fourth Malaysia Plan, 24.8 per cent of the Bumiputra equity (that is 30 per cent of the countries total equity) would be held by Bumiputra trust agencies. With the NEP raising Bumiputra expectations, it is imperative that these holdings are transferred to the Bumiputra individuals as rapidly as possible. The Amanah Saham Nasional (ASN) Scheme is the first giant step in that direction. However, a more global scheme than the ASN is required to ensure that this equity is transferred to the Bumiputra individuals, and will remain and grow with these individuals, resulting in a massive spin-off in entrepreneurial development. Only then could the Bumiputra equity expand, and multiply by itself, without having to depend forever on massive public sector assistance.

Since the achievement of the NEP targets is within the context of the expanding economy, the international environment is crucial in determining the achievement of these targets. The main source of growth, for the Malaysian manufacturing sector up to 1990, is projected to be the export sector. It is clear from table 2.5 that the export sector is estimated to provide about 37.4 per cent of the total sources of growth for the Peninsular Malaysia industrial sector over the period 1970–90, a percentage higher than that of import substitution or private consumption.

In the coming decade, the growth rate of the industrial world, as exemplified by the OECD countries, is projected to be 2.8 per cent in comparison with 3.2 in the past two decades.[5] This means that the opportunities for the export-market in the 1980s will be substantially less than that which existed in the last decade. This is true for commodities like rubber and palm oil and for light industrial goods (like electrical and electronics components), which have contributed to the Malaysian industrial development in the past decade.

A redeeming feature for the country, however, is that it is located near the Far East which is projected to be the fastest growth area in the coming decade. Malaysia's trading pattern has been increasingly shifting away from the West towards the Far East.[6] If Malaysia could continue to exploit this trend, and build up major markets for its products (especially high technology products) to the Far Eastern market of Japan, Korea, Taiwan, and Hong Kong, it could then minimise the adverse effects of the slower OECD growth rate. In this respect, its 'look East' policy represents a step in the right direction.

However, over the coming decade, Malaysia is expected to face greater competition from the Newly Industrialised Countries (NICs) and other newly industrialising and low-wage countries such as Sri Lanka and Indonesia, in the manufacture and export of industrial

Table 2.5 Peninsular Malaysia: sources of growth in the manufacturing sector, 1970–90

Per cent

	Import substitution	Private consumption	Private investment	Public expenditure	Exports
Processed food	14.3	29.8	0.4	1.2	32.7
Oil and fats	5.1	7.5	0.2	0.3	85.6
Other food	15.8	38.4	0.7	1.6	14.9
Beverages and tobacco	21.1	49.6	0.6	0.5	21.0
Textile and clothing	36.3	20.9	0.5	1.2	31.0
Leather and footwear	11.1	70.7	0	0.4	16.8
Sawmills and furniture	3.5	12.0	11.7	23.0	45.5
Paper and printing	28.0	36.8	3.6	9.0	20.5
Industrial chemicals and fertilisers	42.0	14.5	4.0	3.1	32.0
Chemical products	22.0	36.0	2.8	7.5	28.0
Petroleum refining	27.3	48.7	4.0	9.7	8.0
Rubber processing	3.0	2.8	0.3	0.4	93.8
Rubber products	13.5	44.6	4.4	7.0	30.7
Cement	4.3	8.6	22.5	54.7	0.8
Non-metallic products	22.3	20.4	13.4	32.3	12.3
Ferrous products	3.69	11.2	11.1	18.2	15.2
Non-ferrous products	7.6	4.1	2.3	2.6	5.4
Industrial machinery	48.7	3.0	16.4	10.4	20.0
Electrical machinery	29.5	13.0	9.2	6.6	40.9
Transport equipment	40.8	23.3	14.2	9.5	9.3
Other manufacturing products	31.4	31.6	5.1	5.6	25.9
Total	22.3	20.2	5.0	6.9	37.4

Sources: Malaysia *Third Malaysia Plan 1976–80* Kuala Lumpur: Government Printer, 1976

goods. This competition is expected to be more severe in the 1980s because of a reduction in the surplus of the Malaysian workforce, leading to an increase in the industrial wage rate. The country will find that it will no longer be able to attract labour-intensive industries as successfully, in view of this competition.

It can now be seen that the attainment of continued rapid economic growth in Malaysia hinges crucially on its ability to maintain its political stability, the openness of its economic system, the advancement of its industrial technology, with its consequent ability to compete with the current NICs and the developed world. Malaysia's past tradition in political stability and economic openness essentially means that, unlike the majority of developing countries, it would continue to be a stable and open country. Further, the first step in the technological upgrading has already been undertaken by the successful completion of the Bintulu Liquefied Natural Gas complex, the integrated steel projects and the Malaysian car and motor-cycle projects. If these projects can result in extensive linkages with the consequent upliftment of their technological level and international competitiveness, then there is every possibility that Malaysia can have a thriving industrial sector by 1990, resulting in a thriving diversified economy. Viewed in this light, the heavy industrial projects committed thus far represent bold (though risky) efforts by the government. Nevertheless, these projects have to be undertaken otherwise Malaysia will forever remain an exporter of natural resources without much industrial backbone. With the commitment of these projects, there is at least more than an even chance that Malaysia can achieve its industrial vision of being an advanced NIC by 1990.

3

Infrastructure

The provision of an efficient system of infrastructure is an integral part of the development process in general, and expansion of business in particular. As a whole, the infrastructural system in Malaysia can be described as well developed and more than adequate even relative to the advanced countries. In a world wide comparative study in the late 1950s, Peninsular Malaysia was placed in the second quintile on the technological scale based on 11 infrastructural indicators.[1] The transportation system in particular has been rated as the most advanced in South-East Asia after Singapore.

Much of the development of infrastructure that had taken place before independence was geared towards serving the colonial mercantile economy based mainly on tin and rubber. Investment in infrastructure was thus concentrated on the west coast of Peninsular Malaysia where most of the tin deposits and rubber plantations were located. Inevitably, people migrated to reside in this region, and the pattern of population distribution and geographic obstacles have maintained the inequality in the concentration of infrastructure into the beginning of the 1980s. In order to overcome this inequality, the government has placed increasing emphasis under various development plans to develop the infrastructure in the east coast of Peninsular Malaysia, Sabah and Sarawak.

Road system

The road system of Malaysia consists largely of paved, primary and feeder roads connecting all towns in Peninsular Malaysia and some parts of Sabah and Sarawak (see figure 3.1). By 1983, the total length of roads was estimated to be 38 400 kilometres (km); with about 29 000 km of these in Peninsular Malaysia and the remaining in Sabah and Sarawak. In terms of total length of paved roads as well as

Figure 3.1 Malaysia: distribution of roads and railways systems

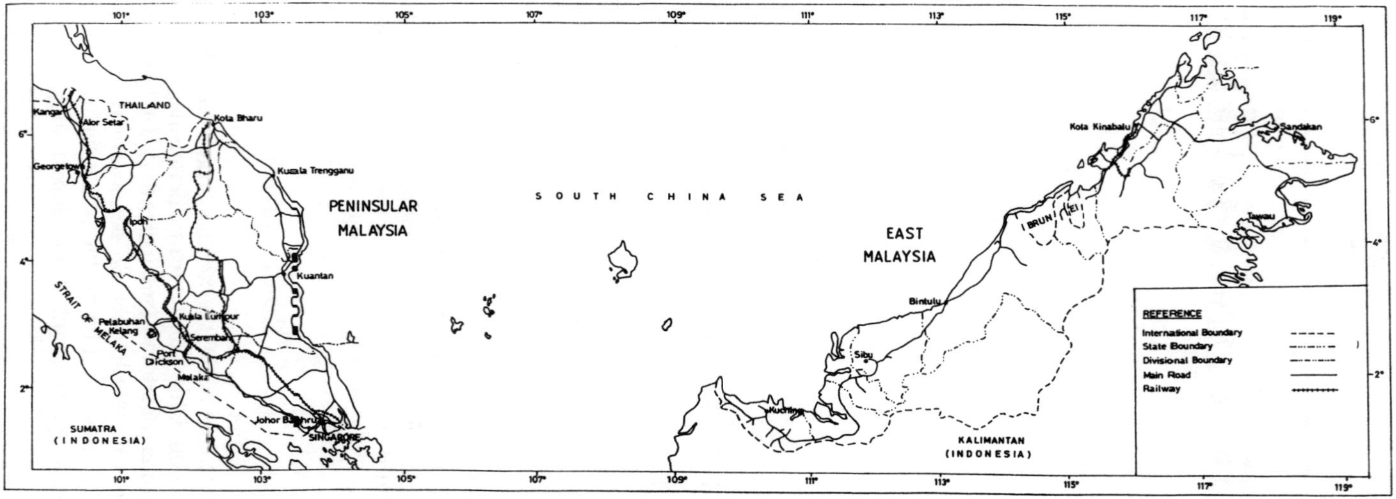

road distance per capita and per vehicle, Malaysia ranks first among the ASEAN countries.

Notwithstanding the relatively well-developed road system, there is a great deal of variation in the distribution of roads among various states of Malaysia. As can be seen from table 3.1, Penang has the highest road density among all the states followed by Malacca and Selangor. The Borneo states of Sabah and Sarawak have the lowest densities. Generally the roads in Peninsular Malaysia are in good condition; although a few of these roads, particularly those in the east coast of Peninsular Malaysia, are occasionally impassible during the monsoon flood seasons occurring from December to January.

A number of major road expansion programmes are currently under implementation. The implementation of road expansion programmes resulted in an increase in the total road network from 29 900 km in 1980 to 38 400 km in 1983. As can be seen from table 3.2, all states benefited from the road expansion programmes with low-income states recording an increase of 37.7 per cent compared with 26.1 per cent for middle-income states and 33 per cent for high-income states. In addition, a total of 1 210 km of major roads were improved and upgraded.

Under the Fourth Malaysia Plan, a total of $M2 650 m. was spent on improving and constructing the road networks in the country. Among the projects implemented were trunk roads, inter-urban expressways and rural roads. Major trunk roads include the Kuala Lumpur-Petaling Jaya Traffic Dispersal Scheme and the Penang Island Traffic Dispersal Scheme, the Johore Port Access Road, the Pantai Barat-Sungai Perak/Lumut Road; and the 1 000 km Sarawak Highway linking Kuching to Miri, as well as the Trans-Borneo Highway to connect Sabah, Sarawak and Brunei.

The inter-urban expressway projects aimed to improve and upgrade the existing north-south road networks. The projects involve the design and construction of a total length of 928 km of north-south expressway stretching from Bukit Kayu Hitam (Kedah) in the north to Johore Bahru in the south, including Penang Island-Mainland Bridge (which will be open to public in September 1985); and a new Klang Valley Expressway linking Port Klang and Kuala Lumpur. On completion, these projects will vastly improve the road system in Malaysia.

The total number of vehicles registered in all states in Malaysia exceeded 3.5 m. units in 1983 with an average growth rate of 11.2 per cent annually (see table 3.2). During the decade of 1970 to 1980, the number of motor vehicles in Peninsular Malaysia grew from 0.7 m. in 1970 to 2.6 m. in 1980, it further increased to 3.5 m. in 1983. The tremendous increase in motor vehicles was mainly motor-cycles and motor-cars. In Sabah the number of motor vehicles grew from 35 000

Table 3.1 Roads by surface type and jurisdiction, 1980 (km)[3]

State	Federal			State			M'CIPAL	Sub-Total		Total[2]
	Paved	Unpaved	Total	Paved	Unpaved	Total	Paved	Paved	Unpaved	
A PENINSULAR MALAYSIA										
1. Perlis	66	27	93	256	87	343	—	322	114	436
2. Kedah	244	13	257	1 702	496	2 198	—	1 946	509	2 455
3. Penang	126	—	126	768	74	842	1 998	2 892	74	2 966
4. Perak	673	8	681	1 915	151	2 066	2 483	5 071	159	5 230
5. Selangor & Federal Territory	581	—	581	1 535	603	2 138	2 169	4 285	603	4 888
6. Negeri Sembilan	508	118	626	1 085	193	1 278	—	1 593	311	1 904
7. Malacca	106	—	106	716	6	722	45	867	6	873
8. Johore	880	198	1 078	1 895	195	2 090	—	2 775	393	3 168
9. Pahang	1 356	829	2 185	1 081	661	1 742	—	2 437	1 490	3 927
10. Trengganu	525	45	570	861	256	1 117	483	1 869	301	2 170
11. Kelantan	259	35	294	779	219	998	204	1 242	254	1 496
Total	5 324	1 273	6 597	12 593	2 941	15 534	7 382	25 299	4 214	29 513
B SABAH*[1]	—	—	—	2 013	6 985	8 998	—	2 013	6 985	8 998
C SARAWAK*[1]	—	—	—	674	1 841	2 515	—	674	1 841	2 515
GRAND TOTAL	5 324	1 273	6 597	15 280	11 767	27 047	7 382	27 986	13 040	41 026

Notes:
1 All roads in the states of Sabah and Sarawak are under state jurisdiction
2 Due to improvement of road surface and reclassification of roads under state and Federal jurisdiction, the total mileage varies between years and will not be consistent
3 Statistics on this date published previously is for the year 1977
*Figures are for 1977

Sources:
1 Road Section, Public Works Department HQ, Kuala Lumpur
2 Public Works Department HQ, Sabah, Kota Kinabalu
3 Public Works Department HQ, Sarawak, Kuching

Table 3.2 Total number of vehicles registered in Peninsular Malaysia, 1980–83

Vehicle type	1980 ('000)	1983 ('000)	Average growth rate (%)
Motor-cycles	1 446	2 029	12.0
Private Motor-cars	843	1 151	10.9
Buses	15	18	6.7
Taxis and hired cars	19	26	11.9
Lorries and vans	190	248	9.3
Others (eg, trailers, hire and drive vehicles)	86	98	4.6
Total	2 598	3 570	11.2

Source: Malaysia *Mid-Term Review Fourth Malaysia Plan, 1981–1985* Kuala Lumpur: Government Printer, 1984

in 1970 to 97 000 in 1980, while the corresponding figures for Sarawak were 39 000 and 126 000 respectively.

The railway system

The total length of railway line in Peninsular Malaysia, including feeder branches linking Prai, Port Weld, Port Dickson, Port Kelang, Teluk Anson and Tumpat, is 1 665 km with 1 065 bridges. Since its completion in 1931, the rail network in the Peninsula has been essentially unchanged. The main railway line runs north from Singapore and then separates into east and west coast lines; these lines connect with the State Railway of Thailand at Padang Besar on the west, and Golok on the east.

The Sabah State Railway runs for a distance of 155 km from Kota Kinabalu to Beaufort and Tenom with an extension to Melalap.

The railway traffic flow reflects closely the pattern of economic activities, with the western line carrying the greatest volume, and the east coast line operating on a level just sufficient to cover running costs. Increasing competition from other modes of transport has slowly reduced the importance of the Malayan Railway since the 1930s. However, the Malayan Railway began implementing its long-term programmes of replacement, rehabilitation and modernisation in 1971. These programmes have resulted in the improvement of the overall performance of the railway, particularly with regard to passenger traffic, which showed an upward trend, increasing from 5.2 m. passengers in 1970 to 7.0 m. in 1980. In terms of passenger-kilometres, this showed an increase from 620 m. to 1 356 m. Freight traffic showed an increase from 1 202 m. tonne-kilometres in 1970 to 1 637 m. tonne-kilometres in 1980.

Malaysian ports

Although there are very few natural ports in Peninsular Malaysia, there are a number of very good semi-manmade ports; the major Malaysian ports are Port Kelang and Penang on the west coast, the new Johore Port at the southern tip of the Peninsula and the new Kuantan Port on the east coast. Other smaller ports are Port Dickson (mainly for petroleum products), Malacca (mainly a lighterage port), and Lumut (a major port) on the west coast and Tumpat on the east coast, which is mainly a fishing port and handles the existing small coastal shipping movement.

In Sarawak, the western coast is a low-lying plain with many slow-moving rivers, some of which are navigable by small coasters. The north-west coast of Sabah has a narrow coastal plain with rapid rivers and offers less suitable sites for ports than the east coast. Notwithstanding the less advantageous of the ports in Sabah and Sarawak, there are few important ports in both states. Examples of those in Sabah are Kota Kinabalu, Sandakan and Tawau; and Kuching, Bintulu in Sarawak.

Apart from the sea-borne transport, the role of river transport in the more isolated areas of Malaysia is also important. Some highly localised boat services are in operation on the rivers of Pahang, Kelantan and Trengganu.

During the last decade, there was a rapid growth in maritime activities. The increase in traffic was particularly significant in Malaysian international trade. By the end of 1980, a total of 16.2 m. tonnes of cargo was handled by the ports in Peninsular Malaysia compared with 7.9 m. tonnes in 1970. In Sabah, a total of 2.8 m. tonnes was handled in 1980 compared with 0.6 m. tonnes in 1970; while in Sarawak, 2.9 m. tonnes was handled in 1980 compared with 1.6 m. tonnes in 1970.

Nearly all the entrepôt and import-export trade of Malaysia is carried on by ships. More than 85 per cent of Malaysia's total cargo passed through Peninsular Malaysian ports. Table 3.3 shows that in 1980, Port Kelang and Penang handled over 36 per cent and 25 per cent respectively of Malaysia's total cargo. The ports of Sabah and Sarawak altogether handle less than 30 per cent of the total; the bulk of this being timber exports. With the steady growth in the Malaysian economy and the consequent expansion in international trade, the number of ships arriving at and departing from Peninsular Malaysia ports increased from 11 000 in 1964 to 29 000 in 1978.

The Malaysian International Shipping Corporation (MISC), the national shipping line, continued its fleet expansion and diversifica-

Table 3.3 Cargo handled by Malaysian ports, 1980 (thousand tonnes)

Port	Tonnage handled	%
Port Kelang	8 000	36.5
Penang port	5 600	25.6
Johore port	2 200	10.0
Other Peninsular ports	400	1.8
Sarawak ports	2 900	13.2
Sabah ports	2 800	12.8
Total	21 900	100.0

Source: Malaysia *Fourth Malaysia Plan 1981–85* Kuala Lumpur: Government Printer, 1982, 319–20

tion programmes during the decade 1971–80. By the end of 1980, it owned and operated a diversified fleet of 31 vessels with a total tonnage of 814 000 dead weight.

The total cargo tonnage expected to be handled by the ports in Peninsular Malaysia is estimated to increase from 16.2 m. tonnes in 1980 to 25.5 m. tonnes in 1985, giving an annual growth rate of 9.5 per cent. In Sabah, the total cargo tonnage is expected to increase from 2.8 m. tonnes to 4.9 m. tonnes while in Sarawak, the corresponding increase is expected to be from 2.9 m. tonnes to 6.5 m. tonnes, giving an annual growth of 11.8 per cent and 17.5 per cent, respectively.

With the completion of three general cargo wharves, dolphin wharves, dry and liquid bulk terminals, the handling capacity of Port Kelang will be increased to 13.9 m. tonnes per annum by the end of 1985. The capacity of Penang Port will be increased to 12.9 m. tonnes per annum, with the implementation of a container project at North Butterworth and an additional berth to the existing bulk cargo terminal.

The expansion of Johore Port, scheduled for completion by 1983, comprises the extension of the existing marginal wharf to provide for an additional multi-purpose ocean berth for general cargo as well as containers and two berths for dry bulk cargo. The completion of these facilities together with the lighterage wharf, dangerous cargo-jetty and other ancillary on-shore facilities will increase the total cargo handling capacity of the port from 3.5 m. tonnes to 7.6 m. tonnes per annum.

The construction of the Petroleum Supply Base in Kemaman, Trengganu, to meet the requirements of petroleum exploration activities was completed in 1982. The project consists of terminal shore facilities, a harbour basin of 120 metres width and an approach channel of nine metres draught, sufficient to accommodate supply ships of 5 000 dead weight tonnes.

There were also plans for expansion of the ports both in Sabah and Sarawak. For instance, in Sabah, the expansion of Tawau Port involving the provision of four additional berths and the Sepangar Bay industrial jetty had been completed. With this expansion, it allows Tawau Port to provide an additional 900 000 tonnes of general cargo handling capacity. The expansion of Kota Kinabalu and Sandakan ports which include the extension of wharves, construction of container freight stations and installation of container handling equipment. With this expansion, the capacity of Kota Kinabalu Port is expected to increase from 0.9 m. tonnes to 2.5 m. tonnes per annum, while that of Sandakan Port will increase from 0.6 m. tonnes to 1.2 m. tonnes per annum. In Sarawak, the Bintulu Port Project was completed in 1982. Besides catering for general and bulk cargo, it also provides specialised facilities for handling liquefied natural gas (LNG), ammonia and urea. The second phase of expansion of the Kuching Port was also completed.

Air transport

Malaysia had eighteen airports at the beginning of the 1980s, of which nine are in Peninsular Malaysia, five in Sabah (including a military airbase in Labuan) and four in Sarawak. Kuala Lumpur (Subang), Penang, Johore Bahru (Senai), Kota Kinabalu and Kuching airports have facilities for international air traffic, while the rest cater for domestic flights, operated mainly by the government-owned Malaysian Airline System, which has a fleet of 38 aircrafts of varying sizes. The Kuala Lumpur (Subang) International Airport handles about 40 per cent of the total air passengers and 54 per cent of the total air cargo for the whole of Malaysia (see table 3.4) and is undoubtedly the most important airport for the country. The Penang Airport, since the completion of the renovation programme, has begun to acquire increasing importance in international air traffic and is now generally regarded as the northern gateway to Malaysia. In Sabah and Sarawak, air travel is the most important mode of transport for incoming visitors and for domestic businessmen.

The last decade marked a rapid growth in the development of civil aviation and air transportation in the country. In Peninsular Malaysia, passenger traffic increased from 0.8 m. in 1970 to 3.5 m. passengers in 1980, showing an annual growth rate of 15.8 per cent. In Sabah, it increased from 54 800 to 1.7 m. passengers and in Sarawak, from 0.4 m. to 1.3 m. passengers, giving an annual growth rate of 26 per cent. Freight traffic in Sabah during the same period,

Table 3.4 Air traffic at Malaysian airports, 1981

Number of passengers ('000)			**Number of landings/take-offs ('000)**			Mail hanlded ('000 kilos)			Cargo ('000 kilos)		
Embarked	Disembarked	Total	Internal flight	International flight	Total	Landed	Despatched	Total	Landed	Despatched	Total
2 422	2 369	4 791	62.35	37.29	99.64	2 134	2 734	4 868	19 169	19 431	38 600

Source: Peninsular Malaysia *Monthly Statistical Bulletin, Mar. 1983* Kuala Lumpur: Department of Statistics, 1983, 105–6

increased from 5 070 to 9 106 tonnes and in Sarawak, from 2 186 to 7 500 tonnes, giving an annual growth of 6 per cent and 13.1 per cent respectively.

The Malaysian Airline System (MAS) expanded and upgraded its domestic and international services with the expansion of its fleet size from 22 in 1972 to 27 in 1980 by the replacement of three B707 with three Airbuses; the acquisition of one F27, two B737s and two DC10s (in 1982, it also acquired two B747s); as well as the increase in landing rights as a result of the signing of new air service agreements. In addition, MAS continued to give priority to rural air services in Sabah and Sarawak with the number of aerodromes served increasing from 17 in 1972 to 25 in 1980.

As a result of this expansion, MAS carried a total of 3.5 m. passengers in 1979/80 compared with only 1.9 m. passengers in the second year of its operation in 1973/74. The carriage of cargo also showed a significant increase from 9 400 tonnes to 81 600 tonnes, giving it an annual growth rate of 43.5 per cent.

During the coming decade, the passenger and cargo traffic is expected to grow at a rate of 10 per cent and 15 per cent per annum respectively. The international passenger traffic growth is expected to grow faster than that of domestic traffic. To meet this growth, the development programme for civil aviation will include expansion and improvement of airports, provision of navigational aids, installation of additional facilities for the Flight Information Region (FIR) and the establishment of a Civil Aviation Training College. In terms of fleet development, MAS will continue to acquire more aircrafts to improve further the capacity and frequency of both domestic and international services.

Public utilities

Electricity

The demand for electricity in Peninsular Malaysia showed an annual growth of about 12.7 per cent; increasing from about 2.2 m. kilowatt hour (kwh) in 1970 to 7.3 m. kwh in 1980. The average consumption in Peninsular Malaysia was 545 kwh per person. The development of hydro-electric power generation was given emphasis during the Third Malaysia Plan (1976–80),[2] but due to its long gestation period, the major source of power generation is still through thermal plants using fuel oil. The electricity generated by the National Electricity Board (NEB) from its thermal, hdyro and gas power stations was estimated at 770 Megawatts (Mw) in 1970; this increased to 2 140 Mw in 1980. Installed capacity was 2 700 Mw in 1983 to meet increasing demand.

Projects launched under the NEB's ambitious development programme are coming on-line and a new generating capacity of about

2 850 Mw is expected to be installed by 1990. The new capacity will come from the construction of gas turbines at the Connaught Bridge power station, the combined cycle power station at Paka, both phases of the Klang thermal power stations, hydro-power plants at Bersia and Kenering and the multi-purpose hydro-power project at Kenyir.

By 1986, the NEB would be in the position to generate 5 100 Mw, if all projects are on schedule. However, projected demand is only 2 700 Mw due to the temporary slow-down in the economy. The excess capacity will allow for breakdowns and planned maintenance, and the government's emphasis on heavy industrialisation is also expected to generate greater demand for power (for example, when the Hicom car plant and steel plant come into operation).

Another aspect of the NEB's development programme—energy diversification—will result in cost savings and prevent electricity rates from escalating. The NEB has speeded up the utilisation of hydro power, coal and natural gas for power generation. As a result of expected cost savings from these sources compared to fuel oil, there will probably be no rise in electricity prices for the next few years.

With the increased generating capacity, the transmission and distribution systems were also expanded. Transmission lines increased by 83.6 per cent within the period 1970–80, while the distribution of lines increased by 400 per cent within the same period. The transmission network will also be strengthened with more lines linking demand and supply centres, such as that between Kuala Lumpur and the Port Dickson power station, which at present, supplies 60–70 per cent of the Klang Valley's power needs.

During the period 1970–80, 3 621 rural electricity projects, costing about $187.2 m. were implemented in Peninsular Malaysia, while about $37.2 m. was spent on the implementation of rural electricity projects in Sabah and Sarawak.

The industrial and commercial sectors are the largest consumers of electricity, taking about 79 per cent of the total generated in Peninsular Malaysia and 67 per cent in Sarawak, while the domestic sector consumed 14 per cent and 19 per cent respectively.

During the period 1981–85, the government plans to further extend electricity supply especially to the rural areas through the implementation of mini-hydro schemes and solar installations. While 91 per cent of town dwellings are electrified, only 37 per cent of the rural population receive electrical supply. The National and Rural Development Ministry has estimated the cost of electrification of all *kampungs,* to be some $M3.9 billion, on which $M400 m. annual interest will have to be paid. Electrification projects for the rural population are expensive because of the dispersed nature of the *kampungs*. The NEB expects to increase the number of rural households supplied with electricity from 0.8 m. in 1980 to 1.1 m. by 1985. In Sabah, about 270 minor projects and mini-hydro schemes are being planned by the electricity board to supply electricity to 24 000 rural households. In Sarawak, the electricity board intends to widen electricity supply to about 17 000 households through conventional diesel generators, mini-hydro schemes and solar installations.

Water supply

In 1978, the total consumption of tap water in Peninsular Malaysia was 362.4 m. gallons per day. The urban coverage served with portable water increased from 83 per cent in 1970 to 90.7 per cent in 1980 whilst rural coverage improved to 47.2 per cent in 1980 from 39 per cent in 1970. By 1990, it is estimated that 97.1 per cent of the urban population and 83.2 per cent of the rural population in the Peninsular will be supplied with tap water. About $263.8 m. will be allocated for pilot projects to meet this target.

Table 3.5 shows that the majority of the rural population in the less developed states of Kelantan, Trengganu, Kedah and Perlis are still not covered by the water supply system. To balance up the uneven distribution, the federal government has provided interest-free loans to Water Boards in the poor states in order to speed up its rural water supply programmes.

Currently, the Public Works Department has extended the existing network of pipelines as far into the rural areas as they can, while the

Table 3.5 Percentage of total rural and urban population served with piped water in Peninsular Malaysia, 1978

State	Rural (%)	Urban (%)	Consumption (mgd)	Estimated consumption (mgd), 1990
Johore	25	100	42.5	134.0
Negri Sembilan	60	85	19.4	45.0
Selangor	60	87	130.0	250.0
Perak	50	95	60.2	140.4
Kedah	25	86	19.8	100.0
Perlis	—	45	0.7	8.5
Pahang	45	90	15.3	60.0
Trengganu	20	70	4.4	28.2
Kelantan	8	48	4.0	24.3
Malacca	60	98	11.9	32.5
Penang	74	96	54.2	100.0
Peninsular Malaysia	40	88	362.4	922.9

Source: Water Supply Division, Kuala Lumpur: Public Works Department

Table 3.6 Telephone, telex and telegram facilities, Malaysia 1976–81

Year	Telephone ('000)			Telex ('000)		Telegram ('000)	
	Home subscribers	Business subscribers	Total	Subscribers	Capacity	Total sent	Total received
1976	91	103	194	1.5	3.1	n a	n a
1977	112	116	228	1.9	3.6	1 045	625
1978	141	130	271	2.2	4.0	1 203	1 742
1979	178	147	325	3.1	4.0	1 092	699
1980	228	167	396	3.9	5.0	958	497
1981	297	192	489	4.1	5.0	1 120	294

Source: Kuala Lumpur: Telecommunication Department, 1982

The microwave trunk network connects all the urban centres in Peninsular Malaysia. In Sabah and Sarawak, a new microwave trunk telephone network has also been established to link all the main towns. Peninsular Malaysia is linked to Sabah and Sarawak via satellite and the troposcatter system, and also by the recently completed submarine cable between Kuantan and Kuching. Consequently, the whole nation was connected by the Subscriber Trunk Dialing Service (STD) by the end of 1980. This development also facilitated the expansion of the television broadcasting services throughout the country.

Direct telecommunication links are being established to various countries through the use of satellites and submarine cables. The establishment of these direct links facilitated the introduction of the International Subscriber Dialing (ISD). Together, the ISD and the STD enable direct international dialing from practically all the urban centres in the country.

Telex services were expanded during the period 1970–80, as a result of the automation of the services and in response to growing domestic and international demand. This progress led to an increase in the number of telex subscribers from 183 in 1970 to 3 500 in 1980.

Telecommunications development programmes include the improvement and extension of local subscribers network and automatic exchanges as well as trunk and junction network to fulfil the future needs of the country. The target is to install 1.2 m. telephones and to provide telex services for 15 000 subscribers by 1985. To meet this target, computer-controlled SPC (Store Programme Control) exchanges will be installed to increase the existing capacity of 667 000 telephone links to about 1.9 m. in 1985. The automatic telephone network will also be extended to cater for the need of the rural population. The domestic telex services will be improved and more public telephones installed. To improve the capacity and efficiency of the Telecommunication Department, the billing system for the telephone and telex services will be decentralised and further computerised. It is anticipated that by the end of 1985, the number of applicants in the waiting list for telephones will be reduced to 10 per cent compared with about 23 per cent in 1980.

Postal services

The Postal Services Department in Malaysia handles some six billion items a year since the early 1980s, and this increases at a rate of 9 per cent a year. To cater for this increase, 70 post offices have been constructed, 72 old post offices renovated and 156 postal vans purchased since 1980. The rural services of the department have also been expanded with the opening of 152 new postal agencies and 33 mobile post offices.

The department has also started on a large-scale modernisation programme. It has mechanised its postal service (the second South-East Asian country, after Hong Kong to do so) and will be computerising its facilities in stages. A national post code system will be launched by the end of 1984 to ensure faster and more accurate delivery. Another innovation that has been introduced is the facsimile transmission service for the public which was started in mid-1984. Known as Intelpost, the service allows the public to transfer their documents to places within the country and outside within seconds. The facsimile machine has been installed at the General Post Office in Kuala Lumpur, Penang, Ipoh, Johore Baru, Kuala Trengganu, Kuching and Kota Kinabalu. While the service is available to any part of the country, only Hong Kong, Australia (Sydney) and England (London) will be able to receive messages from here. However, plans are underway to extend the service to Japan, Germany, the United States and the United Arab Emirates.[3]

4

Monetary and capital markets

The early development of the financial system in Malaysia was closely associated with the growth of foreign trade and general commerce. Before Independence in 1957, the financial system was dominated by a few foreign banks engaged primarily in the mobilisation of deposits for the financing of exports of natural rubber and tin, imports of food and manufactured goods, as well as domestic trading activities. After Independence, the establishment of the Central Bank (Bank Negara Malaysia) in January 1959 under the Central Bank of Malaysia Ordinance, 1958, marked a new era in the history of money and banking in Malaysia.

The first two decades after independence saw the transition of a Malaysian financial structure that was increasingly geared towards meeting Malaysian needs, particularly the financing of investment in agricultural and manufacturing activities. At the end of 1959, there was a total of 26 banks, of which only eight were Malaysian incorporated banks with a share of only five per cent of the aggregate assets of the banking system. However, by 1982, the banking system had enlarged to 38 banks, of which 22 were domestic banks; the financial system in the country had become relatively diversified and sophisticated, with a population per banking office ratio of approximately 26 000 to 1, which is among the best in the developing world.

Structure of the financial system

The financial system in Malaysia can be divided into two groups: the banking system and the non-bank financial intermediaries. The structure of the financial system is illustrated in figure 4.1.

The banking system

The banking system comprises of the Central Bank (Bank Negara), commercial banks, finance companies licensed as borrowing

Figure 4.1 The Financial system structure as at 31 December 1979

The banking system

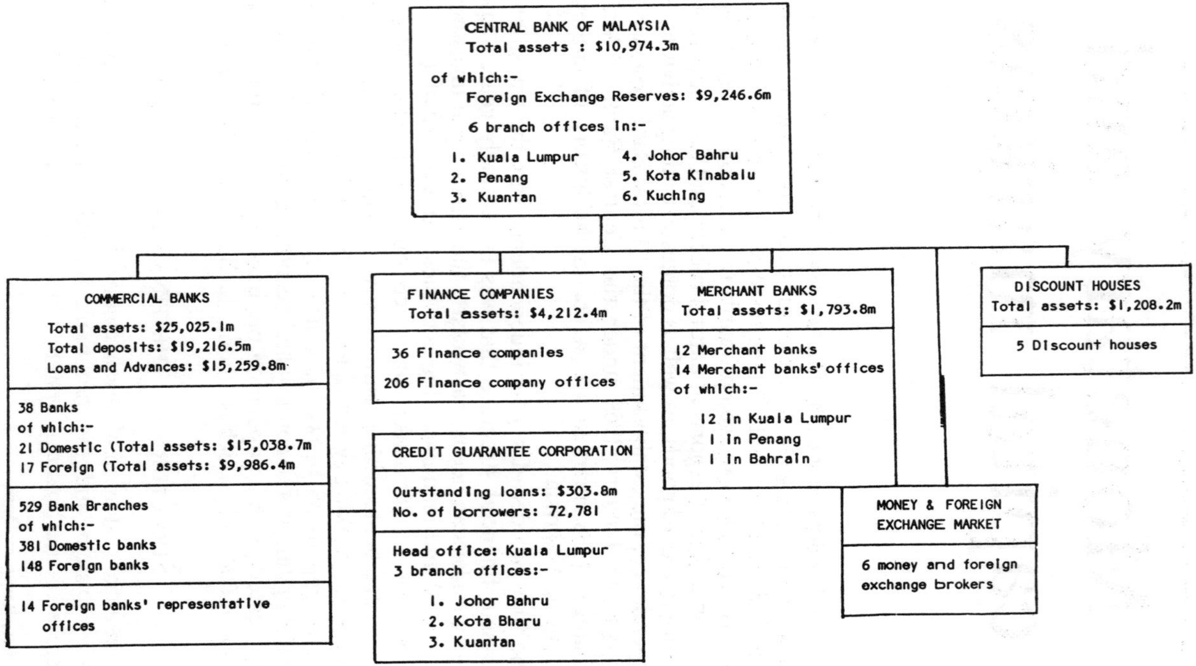

NON-BANK FINANCIAL INTERMEDIARIES

DEVELOPMENT FINANCE INSTITUTIONS
Total assets: $1 469.7m

- Malaysian Industrial Development Finance
- Agricultural Bank of Malaysia
- Borneo Development Corporation
- Sabah Credit Corporation
- Development Bank of Malaysia
- Sabah Development Bank

- Industrial Development of Malaysia Berhad*

SAVINGS INSTITUTIONS

National Savings Bank
Total assets: $1 105.9m
6 Branch offices
7 Regional Public Relations and Marketing offices
616 Post offices with savings facilities

Urban Credit Co-operatives
Total assets: $397m

Rural Credit Co-operatives
Total assets: $70m

Bank Rakyat
Co-operative Central Bank
Housing Co-operatives

PROVIDENT AND PENSION FUNDS
Total assets: $9 310.7m

Employees Provident Fund
Total assets: $7 986.8m
No. of contributors: 3.5m

Teachers Provident Fund
Total assets: $127m
No. of active contributors: 47

Armed Forces Fund
Total assets: $379.7m
No. of contributors: 70,000

130 Other Statutory and Private Provident and Pension Funds
Total assets: $612m
No. of contributors: 65,000

Social Security Organisation
Total assets: $205.2m
No. of contributors: 1.25m

INSURANCE COMPANIES

Total assets: $2 011.5m
of which:-
Life insurance companies $1 325.3m
General insurance companies $686.2m

68 Insurance Companies
of which:-
36 Domestic
32 Foreign

48 General insurance companies
7 Life insurance companies
13 Composite life and general

1 Reinsurance company
1 Export credit insurance company

OTHER FINANCIAL INTERMEDIARIES

Housing Credit Institutions
Total assets: $1 654.7m

Malaysia Building Society

Borneo Housing Mortgage Finance

Housing Loans Division, Treasury

Bumiputra Investment Foundation

Pilgrims Management and Fund Board

Komplek Kewangan Malaysia Berhad

CAPITAL MARKET

UNIT TRUST

5 Unit trust companies
20 Unit trust funds

Size of funds $127.6m
No. of unit holders: 91 623

STOCK EXCHANGES

Kuala Lumpur Stock Exchange
No. of companies listed: 253

Malay Stock Exchange Division of the Komplex Kewangan Malaysia Bhd.
No. of companies listed: 5

Source: Malaysia, *Money and Banking in Malaysia* 1980, Bank Negara Malaysia, 1980
*Established on 7 August 1979

companies and merchant banks. The commercial banks form the core of the system with the Bank Negara at its apex. The principal objectives and functions of the Bank Negara are:

1 to issue currency and to keep reserves safeguarding the value of the currency;
2 to act as banker and financial adviser to the government;
3 to promote monetary stability and a sound financial structure; and
4 to influence the credit situation to the advantage of the country.

To enable the Bank to discharge these responsibilities, Bank Negara is vested with comprehensive legal powers by the Banking Act, 1973, the Borrowing Companies Act, 1969, among others to regulate and supervise the financial system of the country. The major network for mobilisation of domestic savings remain with the commercial banks. This notwithstanding, the role of the commercial banks has also evolved from the traditional one of mobilisation of domestic funds and the using of funds for the financing of trade and commerce to that of motivating and promoting economic development in the country. Further, commercial banks are the only financial institutions licensed by Bank Negara for trading with cheque-paying banks and dealers in foreign exchange.

As stated previously, at the end of 1982, there were 38 commercial banks engaged in accepting deposits, providing checking facilities and making loans and advances.[1] Of these, there were 22 domestic banks, the remaining 16 were foreign banks, with a total of 608 banking officers, centred mainly in the capital, Kuala Lumpur and other major urban areas.

Three major types of deposits are accepted by the commercial banks in Malaysia:

1 current accounts which are non-interest bearing except for some of the large current accounts of Government and statutory authorities, where a low rate of interest is paid;
2 fixed or term deposits which have maturities varying from one month to over 12 months. All such deposits earn interest, which is normally paid annually or on maturity date;
3 saving deposits are also interest bearing, but the rate payable is normally lower than that for fixed deposits.

Besides these deposits, the commercial banks also accept a miscellany of deposits in the form of margins for guarantees and letters of credit. No interest is payable on these deposits.

As a single group, commercial banks provide the largest proportion (about 50 per cent) of credit to the private sector. Lending by the commercial banks is normally made in the form of overdrafts, and loans of varying repayment periods.

The commercial banks are regularly urged by Bank Negara to place more emphasis on term-lending, especially for industrial development, rather than the traditional overdraft arrangement, which is more appropriate for the financing of trade and working capital. Such loans had increased from $M115 million (or 5.8 per cent of total loans and advances) at the end of 1969 to $M15 713 m. (or 43 per cent of the total) at the end of 1983. Trade bill financing constituted 9 per cent of the total loans outstanding at the end of 1983. The sources and uses of commercial bank funds as at the end of 1983 are summarised in table 4.1.

All commercial banks are authorised by Bank Negara to deal in foreign exchange; and inter-bank and merchant rates for all major currencies with respect to the Malaysian *ringgit* are quoted daily. All

Table 4.1 Commercial banks: sources and uses of funds as at 31 December 1983

	$Mm.
Sources	
Capital and reserves	2 994.8
Deposits	37 124.2
Negotiable certificates of deposit issued	3 305.6
Amounts due to financial institutions[1]	2 507.1
Bankers acceptance	1 603.2
Others	6 088.1
Total	53 623.0
Uses	
Cash and clearing balances	617.0
Statutory reserves	1 852.7
Money at call	1 235.3
Amount due from financial institutions[1]	4 216.3
Investments	6 782.1
Treasury bills	2 252.2
Government securities	4 038.9
Private securities	491.0
Foreign securities	39.1
Loans and advances	36 189.8
Fixed assets	694.2
Other	3 195.7
Total	61 604.3

Source: Bank Negara Malaysia Kuala Lumpur: *Annual Report 1983* 1984, 60
Note: [1]Refer to amounts due to and due from other commercial banks, merchant banks and finance companies.

the banks also offer customers the normal foreign exchange services, including the provision of finance for foreign trade by way of documentary letters of credit, discounting of bills of exchange and other standard banking instruments. Following the liberalisation of exchange control regulations on 8 May 1973, all foreign exchange payments abroad for trade services and transfers involving amounts not exceeding the equivalent of $M1 million per day are authorised by the commercial banks on behalf of Bank Negara. Foreign exchange payment exceeding $M1 m. per day are authorised by Bank Negara itself.

Finance companies, licensed as borrowing companies, constitute the second most important institutional source of private sector credit. They operate in the medium-term credit market and are prohibited from accepting deposits which are repayable on demand, dealing in gold or foreign exchange and granting loans in the form of overdrafts. More than 90 per cent of the deposits with the finance companies are in the form of fixed deposits with varying maturities ranging from three months to over a year. On the lending side nearly one-half of finance company lending is directed to hire-purchase financing, mainly for motor vehicles and equipment. Lease financing and factoring of bills, are also acquiring increasing importance among this group of companies. The deposit and lending rates of the finance companies are determined in the market place, and are generally higher than those of the commercial banks.

The sources and uses of the funds of the finance companies as at the end of 1983 are summarised in the table 4.2. In 1982, there were about 41 finance companies operating in 248 offices. The policy of Bank Negara is to grant approval for the opening of new finance company offices in the smaller towns and the rural areas, since the number of such offices in these areas has remained relatively small.

Merchant banking commenced operations in 1970, and there are at present 12 merchant banks, with 15 offices, most of them being joint ventures between Malaysians and foreign interests. Merchant banks are engaged in wholesale banking, primarily acting as intermediaries in the money market and capital market. The activities of the merchant banks may be classified broadly into three types:

1 *Deposits:* Commercial banks and finance companies normally place money for short periods with the merchant banks. Because their main source of funds is from the secondary money market, interest rates paid by the merchant banks on fixed deposits are generally higher than those offered by the commercial banks.
2 *Loans:* Loan operations of the merchant banks range from provision of bridging finance to long-term project loans. The merchant banks also provide refinancing facilities, such as

Table 4.2 Sources and uses of finance company funds as at 31 December 1983

		$Mm.
Sources		
Capital and reserves		577.6
Deposits		9 334.3
Amount due to financial institutions[1]		498.9
Refinancing obligations		1.9
Other		946.5
	Total	11 359.2
Uses		
Cash		10.0
Statutory reserve		179.8
Money at call		396.3
Amount due from financial institutions[1]		2 362.8
Investments		192.0
Treasury bills		17.2
Government securities		166.2
Private securities		8.6
Refinancing facilities		104.0
Loans		7 426.5
Fixed assets		61.9
Other		652.9
	Total	11 578.2

Source: Bank Negara Malaysia Kuala Lumpur: *Annual Report 1983* 70
Note: [1]Refer to amounts due to and due from other finance companies, commercial banks and merchant banks

block discounting of hire-purchase papers, financing of trade bills, syndication of loans. Merchant banks also provide services for the management of investment portfolios on behalf of provident and pension funds, corporations and individuals. A major portion of these funds is invested in stocks and shares and Malaysian Government securities.

3 *Other services* provided by the merchant banks include the underwriting of public share issues, and the provision of corporate financial services including advisory services on acquisitions, company restructuring and capital raising.

The sources and uses of funds of merchant banks as at the end of 1983 are summarised in table 4.3.

Table 4.3 Sources and uses of merchant bank funds as at 31 December 1983

		$Mm.
Sources		
Capital and reserves		294.1
Deposits		3 128.4
Amounts due to financial institutions[1]		405.4
Bankers acceptance		677.1
Other		226.8
	Total	4 731.8
Uses		
Cash		3.1
Statutory reserves		44.6
Money at call		—
Amounts due from financial institutions[1]		289.8
Negotiable certificates of deposit held		44.1
Investments		397.0
Treasury bills		—
Government securities		306.4
Private securities		90.6
Loans		3 603.9
Refinancing facilities		98.5
Fixed assets		18.3
Other		232.5
	Total	5 128.8

Source: Bank Negara Malaysia, Kuala Lumpur: *Annual Report 1983*, 76
Note: [1]Refers to amounts due to and due from other merchant banks, commercial banks and finance companies

Non-banking financial institutions

The major non-banking financial institutions include the National Savings Bank, the Discount Houses and Insurance Companies.

The National Savings Bank (NSB) was established on 1 December 1974 to take over the functions and responsibilities of the former Post Office Savings Bank with the aim of making it a more dynamic financial institution—competing effectively with other private financial institutions—in mobilising savings. The NSB is empowered under the National Savings Bank Act, 1974 to engage in the following major activities: to receive deposits payable on demand or otherwise; to grant loans for housing; to operate giro services and to participate in the equity of companies.

The NSB continues to make use of the wide network of post offices on an agency basis, to provide savings bank facilities to the public. As at the end of 1977, the NSB provided savings bank facilities through 709 post offices throughout the country, of which 219 were mobile units. The number of depositors increased to 4.8 m. at the end of the year 1982.

There are five discount houses operating in Malaysia, the first one being set up in 1963. They perform an important function by providing the private sector with a ready avenue of investment for short-term money. The discount houses accept short-term funds mainly in the form of call money, either overnight or on eight-day call but funds can also be deposited for periods of up to 90 days. The rates of interest paid on these deposits are determined mainly by the yields obtainable on Treasury Bills and Government securities. Since the discount houses are required to invest at least 85 per cent of their funds in Treasury Bills and Government securities with a remaining period to maturity of up to three years, these assets are readily rediscounted by the Central Bank.

The non-bank financial system also includes a host of other institutions which provide medium and long-term credit. This can be classified broadly as follows: (i) provident and pension funds, (ii) insurance companies, (iii) rural credit institutions, including the Agricultural Bank of Malaysia, the Farmers' Organisation Authority, and rural credit cooperative societies, (iv) industrial development finance institutions, including The Malaysian Industrial Development Finance Berhad, the Borneo Development Corporation, the Sabah Credit Corporation and the Development Bank of Malaysia, (v) housing credit institutions; including The Malaysian Building Society Berhad, the Borneo Housing Mortgage Finance Berhad and housing cooperative societies, (vi) urban credit institutions, and (vii) Pilgrim Management and Fund Board.

Sources and directions of loans

Bank Negara has been provided with two major groups of instruments to regulate and coordinate the volume and direction of bank credit which in turn affect the growth of loans and advances. The first group comprises the quantitative instruments that affect the volume bank credit. These are the prescribed lending rates, the rates of interest banks are allowed to pay on their fixed and saving deposits, and the statutory reserve requirement. The second group of instruments comprise those that affect the pattern of credit availability. These include the minimum liquidity ratio which must be maintained by each bank, and the guidelines on loan disbursement to the priority sectors including Bumiputras and small businesses.

There is no compulsion on the commercial banks to maintain a given level of loans and advances to the public sector; though borrowings by the government are required to be given more favourable treatment. For example, when the credit growth ceiling of 20 per cent was imposed on commercial bank loans and advances from 1974 as an anti-inflationary measure, loans to the government and approved government corporations were among the categories not subjected to this ceiling. Secondly, on account of the very low risks involved, the interest charge on commercial bank loans and advances to the public sector had been fixed at a preferential rate which was 0.5 per cent below the prime rate set by Bank Negara.

Loans and advances to the public sector accounted for less than 2.5 per cent of the total loans during the period 1965–82. However, in absolute terms the amount of loans to the government sector has increased significantly; from $M3.0 m. in 1965 to $M183 m. in 1975 and $M935 million by 1983 (see table 4.4).

Loans and advances from commercial banks accounted for about 50 per cent of the total resources utilised for the financing of the domestic private sector. The main instruments used to promote commercial bank loans and advances to the private sector are moral persuasion, the prescription of guidelines by Bank Negara, the establishment of institutions to support the objectives of these credit prescriptions, changing the composition of the minimum liquidity ratio and specifying the eligible assets to be held against savings deposits.

In order to achieve the objectives of the NEP, emphasis was placed on employment creation, faster economic growth and a more equitable distribution of income and opportunities among the races. To achieve these objectives, guidelines were issued by Bank Negara to ensure that more loans would be granted to the agricultural and manufacturing sectors and to priority sectors such as the Bumiputra community and small-scale enterprises.

In the past, commercial banks had avoided involvement with small-scale enterprises, due to the lack of acceptable collateral for the loans from these enterprises. To compensate for the possibly higher rate of defaults, compared with other borrowers, a partial guarantee on the loans extended by the banks to these small borrowers was made by the government with the creation of the Credit Guarantee Corporation (CGC) in 1972. This corporation had launched the General Guarantee Scheme (GGS) in 1973 to provide guarantee cover for loans given by commercial banks to small enterprises in agriculture, commerce and industry.

In 1981, the activities of the CGC was expanded significantly by the launching of the Special Loan Scheme (SLS). The Scheme was designed to provide loans to the really small enterprises at a lower cost. Small-scale enterprises in this case include all registered businesses (as well as petty traders, hawkers and others licensed to trade) with net assets up to $M250 000. In 1982, loans approved for

Table 4.4 Commercial banks: classification of loans and advances

End of period	Agriculture	Mining and quarrying	Manufacturing	Electricity	General commerce[1]	Building and construction	Real estates	Housing	Transport, storage and communication	Financing insurance and building	Miscellaneous[2]	Total loan and advances $Mm.	Of which: loans to government
1965	97.5	31.9	174.2	n.a.	423.7	83.4	n.a.	n.a.	7.7	28.6	294.1	1 141.1	3.0
1970	240.3	51.2	465.6	n.a.	756.1	206.5	n.a.	n.a.	17.4	79.5	543.0	2 359.6	0.3
1975	483.8	106.7	1 265.6	n.a.	1 722.2	480.2	241.5	500.9	89.9	415.3	1 162.3	6 468.4	182.9
1980	1 648.4	210.5	4 693.8	278.9	4 644.2	1 406.6	1 710.2	2 232.4	400.1	1 297.3	2 508.7	21 031.1	324.1
1982	2 134.4	494.5	6 190.0	143.7	6 137.9	1 859.7	3 660.0	3 497.8	715.2	2 739.9	2 092.5	29 665.6	427.3
Sept. 1983	2 346.7	551.7	7 165.5	91.3	7 027.7	2 275.9	4 377.1	3 954.7	699.3	3 575.7	2 702.8	34 768.4	935.2

Source: Malaysia *Money and Banking in Malaysia* Kuala Lumpur: Bank Negara Malaysia, 1984

[1]Data up to December 1979 includes bills discounted or purchased and bills receivable. As from December 1980, such bills have been classified according to group of borrowers and included in the data for the appropriate group

[2]Data up to December 1979 includes loans to the Federal and State Governments. As from December 1980, such loans have been classified according to economic activity and included in data for the appropriate activity

guarantee by the Corporation amounted to $M519.2 m. for a total of 16 958 loans.

In view of the emphasis on loans given to small-scale enterprises, it would be interesting to see what groups and activities have benefited from this policy. During 1973–76, 68 per cent of the loans approved by the Corporation for guarantee under the Scheme were to Malays and 27 per cent to Chinese. These percentages indicate that the CGC had opened up substantial opportunities for the Malay borrowers who would not otherwise have obtained loans without the Scheme. As at the end of 1982, out of the 52 per cent of the total gross loans, twelve were granted to the Bumiputra community.

The pattern of lending of commercial bank loans for guarantee by the Corporation is set out in table 4.5. The bulk (75 to 81 per cent) of the value of the loans approved each year during 1973–82 was for small business. Under the small busines category there are activities such as general commerce; sundry retail trade; transport and motor repair; and building and construction. Agricultural activities accounted for 9 to 19 per cent of the value each year during the period 1973–79 and decreased to about 6 to 7 per cent during the period 1981–82.

Direction of bank lending

Table 4.6 shows the direction of bank lending for the period 1969–82. In accordance with the general guidelines on lending laid down by the Central Bank, special emphasis was given by the commercial banks on lending to the priority sectors of the economy, namely manufacturing, agricultural food production, the Bumiputra community, small borrowers and individuals for purchase of residential houses.

From table 4.6 we can see that these guidelines have been followed by the commercial banks. A substantial proportion of their total credit have been channelled to the financing of manufacturing, general commerce, building construction and property development, including end-financing for the purchase of houses and agriculture. These sectors took up about 75 per cent of the domestic loans in 1982.

Direction of bank lending to the Bumiputra community is shown in table 4.7. Loans and advances granted to Bumiputra individuals and Bumiputra-controlled enterprises rose sharply over the period 1979–82. Bank credit extended to the Bumiputra community amounted to $M2 650 m. (or 17.4 per cent of the total bank loans and advances) in 1979 to $M7 027.3 m. (or 23.7 per cent of the total bank loans and advances) in 1982. Bank credit to the Bumiputra community in all sectors of the economy also showed increases during the period 1979–82. This is a result of specific steps taken to ensure that the Bumiputra community had ready access to credit at reasonable cost.

Table 4.5 Bank lending under the general guarantee scheme and special loan scheme

	Amount approved ($Mm.)													
	GGS[1]		GGS		GGS		GGS		GGS	SLS[2]		GGS	SLS	
	1973		1975		1977		1979		1981			1982		
Small business	9.6	(81.4)	97.3	(77.3)	64.5	(72.4)	100.9	(70.8)	19.9	385.1	(77.3)	7.6	411.6	(79.2)
Of which:														
Building and construction	3.0	(25.4)	17.8	(14.1)	8.5	(9.5)	13.9	(9.8)	2.6	37.9	(7.7)	0.8	40.7	(8.0)
Sundry retail trade	1.9	(16.1)	13.2	(10.5)	8.9	(10.0)	14.9	(10.5)	2.6	49.3	(9.9)	0.9	60.4	(11.8)
General commerce	1.3	(11.0)	18.1	(14.4)	10.6	(11.9)	12.6	(8.8)	3.5	77.0	(15.4)	1.0	75.2	(14.7)
Transport and motor repairs	0.6	(5.1)	6.6	(5.2)	9.0	(10.1)	11.3	(7.9)	2.4	50.4	(10.1)	1.2	58.0	(11.4)
Small-scale industries	1.1	(9.3)	14.8	(11.8)	9.5	(10.7)	14.0	(9.8)	3.1	78.0	(15.5)	1.3	66.0	(13.5)
Of which:														
Food, drinks and tobacco	0.1	(0.8)	3.4	(2.7)	2.0	(2.2)	3.1	(2.2)	0.5	11.1	(2.2)	0.3	10.7	(2.1)
Timber products and furniture	0.1	(0.8)	2.2	(1.7)	2.0	(2.2)	2.2	(1.5)	0.3	11.9	(2.3)	0.2	11.9	(2.3)
Textiles and clothing	0.1	(0.8)	1.9	(1.5)	1.3	(1.5)	1.6	(1.1)	0.6	7.6	(1.5)	0.1	6.1	(1.2)
Building materials	0.3	(2.5)	4.0	(3.2)	1.1	(1.4)	3.2	(2.2)	0.7	23.4	(4.6)	0.3	15.0	(2.9)
Printing and publishing	0.1	(0.8)	1.5	(1.2)	0.7	(0.8)	1.8	(1.3)	0.3	7.1	(1.4)	0.2	8.1	(1.6)
Agriculture	1.1	(9.3)	13.7	(10.9)	15.1	(16.9)	27.6	(19.4)	2.7	35.1	(7.2)	0.7	32.0	(7.3)
Of which:														
Padi cultivation and marketing	0.6	(5.1)	1.9	(1.5)	3.5	(3.9)	5.2	(3.6)	0.5	4.7	(0.9)	0.1	5.8	(1.1)
Livestock and poultry farming	0.1	(0.8)	5.1	(4.0)	4.7	(5.3)	8.0	(5.6)	1.0	13.8	(2.8)	0.2	11.7	(2.3)
Fisheries	0.1	(0.8)	2.3	(1.8)	1.6	(1.8)	2.2	(1.5)	0.2	3.2	(6.5)	0.2	2.9	(0.6)
Total	11.8	(100.0)	125.8	(100.0)	89.1	(100.0)	142.5	(100.0)	25.7	498.2	(100.0)	9.6	509.6	(100.0)

Source: The Credit Guarantee Corporation (CGC)
Malaysia *Bank Negara Malaysia, Annual Reports* Kuala Lumpur: Government Printer, various year

Note: [1]General Guarantee Scheme
[2]Special Loan Scheme
Figures in bracket are in %

Table 4.6 Direction of commercial bank lending

	$Mm. As at end of							
	1970	1972	1974	1976	1978	1980	1982	1983
Agriculture of which	240.3	347.5	416.5	535.8	870.8	1 648.4	2 134.4	2 389.5
Forestry & logging	62.7	159.8	216.3	207.7	330.9	536.6	730.4	770.2
Oil palm	43.1	45.6	51.9	101.5	150.8	385.2	478.8	499.1
Cocoa	—	—	—	—	—	138.9	328.1	392.2
Livestock	—	—	—	—	—	—	153.5	187.3
Rubber	114.5	123.9	109.8	135.5	150.8	587.7	—	206.6
Mining & quarrying of which	51.2	72.0	97.9	105.7	128.1	210.5	494.5	626.3
Tin	—	—	—	—	—	145.2	201.5	—
Crude petroleum & natural gas	—	—	—	—	—	—	171.8	292.2
Quarrying	—	—	—	—	—	32.2	93.0	141.2
Manufacturing of which	465.6	610.3	1 057.0	1 382.0	2 225.4	4 693.8	6 190.0	7 398.8
Processing	—	—	—	—	—	631.8	877.9	1 011.0
Textiles & wearing apparel	—	61.3	150.7	199.5	262.9	552.5	635.0	703.0
Wood & wood products	81.6	67.8	135.6	198.7	297.9	433.4	630.9	755.4
Food	67.9	79.4	104.2	125.5	233.5	409.6	605.4	719.2
Iron & steel products	—	—	—	—	—	—	389.3	462.2
Petroleum products	35.5	37.6	29.3	76.9	129.1	147.3	194.8	368.2
Transport equipment	—	—	—	—	—	255.5	349.8	411.8
Electrical machinery, apparatus & appliances	—	—	—	—	—	236.8	314.2	338.2
Basic metal industries	15.1	6.6	—	—	—	272.9	451.1	601.4
Metal products	99.5	129.0*	203.6	249.2	364.2	280.3	329.7	334.6
Electricity	—	—	—	—	—	278.9	143.7	96.3
Real estate & construction	206.5	240.2	628.7	803.3	1 349.8	3 116.8	5 519.7	7 160.1
General commerce	756.0	724.9**	936.8	1 178.1	1 833.2	4 644.2	6 137.2	7 270.9
Transport and storage	—	—	—	—	—	400.1	715.2	750.1
Financing, insurance and business services	—	—	665.2	994.2	1 446.4	1 297.3	2 739.8	4 074.9
Individual housing loans	376.9	566.3	951.8	668.1	1 229.4	2 234.4	3 497.6	4 157.7
Other	263.1	385.7	634.5	1 269.0	1 572.6	2 508.6	2 093.1	2 857.2
Total loans	2 359.6	3 179.3	5 575.6	8 061.4	12 288.5	21 031.0	29 665.2	36 781.1

Source: Malaysia *Bank Negara Annual Report* Kuala Lumpur: Government Printer, various years
Note: *Includes also machinery
**Includes local trade bills

Table 4.7 Direction of bank lending to Bumiputra community, 1979–82

Item	1979		1980		1981		1982	
	$m	%	$m	%	$m	%	$m	%
Agriculture	205.5	6.85	363.7	9.3	532.8	10.1	685.3	9.8
Mining and quarrying	33.6	1.12	64.7	1.7	84.6	1.6	108.7	1.5
Manufacturing	318.9	10.63	437.9	11.2	586.0	11.1	841.2	12.0
Real estate and construction	541.2	18.03	916.8	23.6	1 337.6	25.4	1 933.8	27.5
General commerce	297.5	9.91	446.3	11.5	599.3	11.4	871.3	12.4
Transport and storage			77.2	1.9	112.5	2.1	154.1	2.2
Financing, insurance and business services	699.2	23.30	259.6	6.7	550.6	10.5	803.1	11.4
Individual housing loans	351.0	11.70	504.3	13.0	677.0	12.9	874.1	12.4
Other	341.0	11.36	620.6	15.9	497.9	9.5	259.9	3.7
Trade bills	213.1	7.10	201.4	5.2	228.8	5.4	369.9	5.3
Total[1]	3 001.0	100.0	3 892.5	100.0	5 264.1	100.0	7 027.3	100.0

Source: Malaysia, Bank Negara Malaysia *Annual Reports* various years
Note: [1]Refer to only Bumiputra individuals and Bumiputra-controlled enterprises
Exclude government agencies and government-controlled corporations

Money market

The Kuala Lumpur money market through which users of funds could borrow from clients having an excess of funds, consists of both the primary and secondary market. The participants in the primary market for short-term funds are the initial suppliers of funds and the final users. The suppliers deposit their surplus funds, in either short-term deposits or current accounts and savings accounts with the commercial bank and other intermediaries. The final users borrow funds from these financial intermediaries in the form of term loans, overdrafts and mortgages. The secondary market or inter-bank market is the channel through which financial institutions which are in need of funds can borrow from other financial intermediaries which have excess funds. Over the past two decades, the size of the inter-bank market has expanded rapidly, reflecting to a large extent better management of funds among the banks. In 1967, the year when the Malaysian dollar was issued to replace the Malayan dollar, the average monthly borrowing on the inter-bank market was $M107 m. By 1982, this had increased to $M4.3 billion a month.

Apart from the inter-bank market, the commercial banks and financial companies often place deposits with the merchant banks which are allowed to accept such deposits at market determined rates. At the end of 1982, deposits of commercial banks and financial companies amounted to $M1.6 billion or 75 per cent of the total deposits with the merchant banks. In addition, the financial companies also maintained substantial deposits with the commercial banks. In 1982, this amounted to $M1.6 billion. All the three types of financial institutions namely, the commercial banks, finance companies and merchant banks are important sources of overnight deposits for the discount houses.

The five discount houses in operation at present are the only financial institutions specialising in short-term money market operations. However, at least 85 per cent of the funds from the deposits must be invested in treasury bills and other Government Bills with maturity of not more than three years. The balance can be invested as Bankers Acceptances and Negotiable Certificates of deposit.

The presence of various forms of financial intermediaries all under the control of Bank Negara provides for the smooth operation of the primary and secondary market through which users of funds could borrow from others having surplus funds.

The foreign exchange market

In Malaysia, all transactions in foreign currency are required to be conducted through anyone of the 38 commercial banks. There are also 220 money-changers who are authorised to buy and sell foreign currencies and notes. The present exchange control mechanism in Malaysia can be described as liberal and applies uniformly to all countries except South Africa and Israel, for which special restrictive regulations apply. Exchange control is administered by Bank Negara in accordance with the provisions of the Exchange Control Act, 1953. Payment to countries outside Malaysia may be made in any currency other than the currencies of South Africa and Israel. Payment within Malaysia must be made in *ringgit*, the Malaysian currency. All payments including the repatriation of capital and remittances are freely permitted. No permission need be sought for each payment abroad for up to $M10 000. Where individual payment in foreign currency exceeds $M10 000, approval has to be obtained before the payment can be affected. Any commercial bank is authorised to approve the application without reference to Bank Negara, except that:

1 In the case of payment of loans borrowed from non-residents, the borrowing has to be approved by Bank Negara and the payments are consistent with the approved condition.
2 In the case of payment of purchase of shares or immovable properties, the payments are financed with funds which are not borrowed from Malaysia.

All exports in excess of $M5 000 fob can be approved by any authorised bank at the time of shipment. All export proceeds must be repatriated to Malaysia within the time-frame specified by the export contract. With respect to borrowing from non-resident or foreign sources, permission from Bank Negara for all loans in excess of $M100 000 must be obtained. Further, remittances and interests on foreign loans also require approval from Bank Negara. Non-resident controlled companies are permitted to borrow up to $M500 000 in Malaysia. For larger amounts of borrowings, the approval of Bank Negara is required and such approval is normally given, based on the genuine need of the company.

The Kuala Lumpur Stock Exchange

The Kuala Lumpur Stock Exchange (KLSE) is the most active component of the capital market in Malaysia, although the primary funds raised are only a fraction of the amount raised in the Government Securities market in Malaysia. There is another exchange, the Bumiputra Stock Exchange (BSE) which was founded in 1969 to facilitate trading in Bumiputra shares. Since its inception, it continues to trade in only five securities, and hence is a very small exchange.

Share broking was formally organised under the Malayan Stockbrokers Association (MSA) in 1937. The MSA was reorganised into the Malayan Stock Exchange (MSE) in 1960, the Stock Exchange of Malaysia (SEM) in 1963; and the Stock Exchange of Malaysia and Singapore (SEMS) in 1965. In 1973, the SEMS split into two exchanges, the Stock Exchange of Singapore (SES) and the Kuala Lumpur Stock Exchange (KLSE), when the currency partly agreement between the two countries was terminated. However, stocks traded on the SEMS are concurrently listed on both exchanges.

The KLSE has expanded rapidly. The turnover has increased from a total of 415 m. units ($M759 m.) in 1974 to 1 038 m. units ($M3 190 m.) in 1982. In terms of market capitalisation, the total market value of listed stocks has grown from $M12.530 m. at the close of 1973 to $M32.484 billion at the close of 1982. This phenomenal growth is attributed to the reasonably high economic growth sustained by the nation during this period.

The KLSE has classified its listed stocks into eight sectors, namely Industrials, Finance, Hotels, Properties, Oil Palms, Dollars Rubber, Sterling Rubber and Tin. It would be informative to go through the elements of this growth sectorally. Table 4.8 summarises the distribution of the annual turnover by sectors during the period 1974 to 1982. It is apparent from this table that the industrial sector has consistently contributed the largest proportion of the total turnover both in terms of volume and value. The finance sector (classified in 1974) has steadily grown to be the second leading sector, while the sterling rubber sector has diminished in importance after 1979.

Table 4.9 exhibits the composition and market capitalisation of these sectors as at the close of 1973 and 1982. The leading position of the industrial sector is once again emphasised. While the number of securities listed as industrials has increased only from 141 to 149, the total market value has risen phenomenally from $M8.726 million to $M5.627 billion. This more than compensated for the reclassification of some securities to finance in 1974. The decline in relative importance of the sterling rubber is generally attributable to the delisting of some 16 securities by 1982. For the tin sector, consolidation of existing companies via mergers resulted in a decrease in the composition from 41 securities in 1973 to 29 in 1982. In the overall perspective, the total number of securities listed at the exchange has remained stable from year to year. The growth in market capitalisation and turnover can thus be attributed to the intensive expansion and consolidation of the listed companies.

In terms of activity, it has been said that a small proportion of stocks are traded on a day-to-day basis on the KLSE. One way to portray market activity is via the number of securities that advanced, declined or remained unchanged. Table 4.10 summarises the daily average proportions for the period 1974 to 1978. It can be observed that the total proportion of securities that are not traded or have remained unchanged is significant during this period.

Table 4.8 Annual turnover of stocks and shares at the Kuala Lumpur Stock Exchange

	Period								
	1974	1975	1976	1977	1978	1979	1980	1981	1982
Volume: (in m.)									
Total	415.4	608.8	420.6	567.9	1 083.6	621.8	1 428.1	1 595.7	1 038.2
Industrials	237.1	318.7	260.4	411.7	642.5	366.2	1 006.8	1 228.4	78.6
Finance	31.9	110.5	77.4	58.6	82.9	40.2	105.7	59.2	59.8
Hotels	31.9	53.8	15.0	0.6	45.9	24.5	50.6	56.2	23.5
Properties	72.9	69.8	21.7	30.0	73.7	27.2	81.5	108.9	75.5
Tins	2.9	21.0	5.8	15.5	69.4	32.3	86.9	48.2	45.8
Dollars rubbers	31.9	24.9	36.8	47.7	101.8	81.3	96.4	84.6	55.0
Sterling rubbers	6.8	10.2	3.5	3.7	67.4	50.2	0.2	0.9	0.8
Value: (in m.)									
Total	759.0	1 292.1	995.4	1 003.7	2 489.9	1 596.2	5 461.9	7 941.8	3 190.2
Industrial	512.6	721.3	582.0	672.5	1 451.4	866.1	3 749.3	6 170.9	2 237.6
Finance	49.9	356.3	303.6	146.8	295.6	151.7	546.6	467.9	333.3
Hotels	48.7	55.0	15.0	0.5	51.6	27.7	71.1	171.5	48.1
Properties	71.1	73.3	23.4	40.3	130.1	50.5	292.1	586.6	206.7
Tins	8.9	34.3	11.6	57.7	170.5	136.4	431.4	220.0	134.9
Dollars rubbers	49.9	32.5	49.2	71.6	230.3	252.3	368.2	323.4	128.5
Sterling rubbers	17.8	19.3	10.5	14.2	160.3	113.5	3.1	1.5	1.1

Source: Compiled from primary records kept by the Kuala Lumpur Stock Exchange

Table 4.9 Composition and market capitalisation of securities at the KLSE (by sectors)

Sectors	No. of securities listed End-1973	No. of securities listed End-1982	Total market value ($m.) End-1973	Total market value ($m.) End-1982
Industrial	141	149	8.726	5 627.149
Finance	—	16	—	10 777.360
Hotels	16	11	0.906	3 010.126
Properties	14	14	0.685	3 907.198
Oil palms	8	10	0.414	3 436.693
$Rubber	24	30	0.621	3 438.844
£Rubber	18	2	0.553	88.688
Tins	41	29	0.625	2 198.230
Total	262	261	12.530	32 484.288

Source: KLSE Gazette Jan. 1974 & Jan. 1983

Table 4.10 Average proportions of advances/declines/unchanged (total stocks: 289)

%	Mean	Standard deviation
Advances	11.79	7.79
Declines	12.79	7.33
Unchanged	75.41	5.70
Total	100.00	

In contrast, only about 25 per cent of the stocks at the NYSE remain unchanged/not traded on a day-to-day basis.[2] The main implication of this observation is that the bid-ask spread can be expected to vary greatly between the stocks. Further, we can anticipate large price changes when less active stocks are traded. In terms of sectors,[3] the property sector remained active from 1974 to 1980, with oil palms emerging as an active sector in 1979. The industrial and finance sectors have played less important roles during this period.

The importance of the KLSE in relation to the world's stock markets can be seen from table 4.11. At the close of 1980, the North American Stock Markets constituted the largest unit in the world. The Asian/Pacific Group was next in importance followed by the European Group; and KLSE, by far, is the smallest of the East/Pacific group.

Table 4.11 Market capitalisation of world stock markets

	1979	*1980*
United States (NYSE)	960	1 285
Canada	98	120
North America	1 058	1 405
Belgium	13	10
Switzerland	44	46
United Kingdom	142	200
Germany	80	74
Holland	24	27
France	54	57
Italy	13	25
Europe	370	439
Australia	39	59
Hong Kong	23	36
Japan	274	336
Singapore	14	24
Malaysia	11	19
East Asia/Pacific	361	474

Source: L. Nasir 'A Study of Market Efficiency and Risk Return Relationship in the Malaysian Capital Market' Doctoral Dissertation, Katholieke Universiteit Leuven, 1983, 24

The KLSE is indeed a small exchange in comparison to most established exchanges. Given the relatively younger existence, the relatively smaller turnover, and the low activity of most stocks, it has often been speculated that the KLSE may not be very efficient in marking prices of securities.

The KLSE has also undergone some recent changes in its operations to upgrade its facilities and management. The stock exchange has been computerised for greater efficiency in the clearing of scripts and more stringent rules are now in use to cut down on excessive speculation in the stock market. Its purpose is to allow it to grow at a healthy pace. Computerisation of trading activities has been planned for the near future.

THE KUALA LUMPUR COMMODITY EXCHANGE

The Kuala Lumpur Commodity Exchange (KLCE) commenced operations in 1980. It was planned as a multi-commodity exchange; trading in rubber, palm oil, tin, pepper and tropical timber, and was part of the Malaysian Government's plan of establishing an international trading centre in Malaysia. Except for pepper, Malaysia is the leading producer and exporter of the commodities mentioned. A futures market for palm oil was the most urgently needed to provide both the producers and refiners of palm oil with an avenue for hedging against violent price fluctuations. At present, palm oil is traded both on the physical (cash) and futures market; and rubber and tin are planned for the near-future.

The KLCE is owned and operated by members who comprise producers, refiners, traders, processors, dealers and others. The exchange is a non-profit making organisation and is not in the business of buying and selling commodity futures. It provides facilities and establishes Rules and Regulations for equitable trading in commodities futures. Membership on the KLCE is of two categories; full members and trade associates. Only Malaysian firms can apply for full membership while trade associates may be local or foreign domiciled firms. They have to fulfil certain conditions and pay membership, as well as subscription fees.

Besides providing adequate hedging facilities for refiners and exporters against violent price movements at least six months ahead, the exchange also collects and disseminates relevant information about market prices and supply and demand factors affecting these prices, thereby leading to more accurate price forecasts.

The Kuala Lumpur Commodities Clearing House Sdn Bhd (KLCCH) is a separate independent clearing organisation from the KLCE, although it is an integral part of futures trading. The main functions of the KLCCH are to guarantee the fulfilment of contracts between its members and maintain the financial stability and integrity of the market. The KLCCH does this principally by registering all contracts traded on the KLCE, establishing and collecting deposits and collecting daily margins from members with adverse market positions. The KLCCH is a joint venture between the International Commodities Clearing House (ICCH) and several local banks. Companies or firms can apply to become Clearing Members, whether or not they are already Full Members of Trade Associates of the Exchange.

5

Labour and manpower

The working-age population of Malaysia (between 15–64 years of age) comprises 55 per cent of the total population of 13.1 m. in 1980. Almost 39 per cent of the population is below 15 years of age while about 6 per cent are more than 65 years of age.[1] The relatively young population and continued high birth rate indicate that the working-age population in Malaysia will increase further in the years to come. Of the 7.4 m. people in the 15–64 age group, 4.6 m. are in the labour force; the labour force participation rates for males and females are 85 per cent and 42 per cent respectively. During the period 1980–85, the Malaysia labour force is anticipated to grow at the rate of 3.1 per cent per annum, with the growth of the 25–39 age group being most rapid (4.9 per cent per annum).

Estimations of the demand for labour during the period 1980–85, reveals that 861 000 jobs will be created. Of these 8 per cent would be professional and technical workers, 1.5 per cent administrative and managerial workers, 14.1 per cent sales workers and 49.3 per cent production workers. These workers, both skilled and unskilled, professional and administrative, will be required to fulfil the manpower needs of Malaysia's developing economy.[2]

PROFILE AND DEMAND FOR SKILLED AND SEMI-SKILLED MANPOWER

It cannot be denied that a skilled and trained labour force is essential to a country that is experiencing rapid expansion in its manufacturing, construction and services sectors. The government's policy of promoting high value added and heavy industries and its intention to de-emphasise labour-intensive industries, clearly indicate that both skilled and semi-skilled labour will be in great demand in the years to come.

The 1980 Population and Housing Census shows that the employment structure for most economic sectors have changed significantly over the period 1970–80. The focus of employment has shifted from the agricultural sector to the industrial and services sector (table 5.1); in 1970 agriculture employment accounted for 52 per cent of the total workforce, while in 1980 the corresponding figure declined to 41 per cent. The greatest employment growth is experienced in the construction sector—which experienced an annual growth rate of 10.9 per cent—followed by the manufacturing and services sector.

Table 5.1 Distribution of the experienced labour force aged 10 and over by economic group, Malaysia, 1970–80[1]

Industry group	1970 (%)	1980 (%)	1970–80 Average annual growth rate (%)
Agriculture, forestry, hunting and fishing	28	21	0.7
Agricultural products requiring substantial processing	24	20	1.2
Mining and quarrying	2	1	−1.9
Manufacturing	8	13	8.0
Construction	2	5	10.9
Electricity, gas and water and sanitary services	1	1	1.9
Commerce	9	11	5.4
Transport, storage and communication	3	4	4.0
Services	17	22	6.2
Industry not adequately described or not stated	6	2	−5.6
Total (%)	100	100	3.3
Total number ('000)	3 286.6	4 593.2	

Source: Malaysia *Population and Housing Census 1980* Kuala Lumpur: Department of Statistics, 1983

Note: [1]Experienced labour force constitutes all workers who are currently working or have worked before

Table 5.2 shows the occupational profile of some selected industries in Malaysia for the year 1980. In each of the 11 professional and technical industries, professional technical workers form less than 1 per cent of the total workforce for 8 of the 11 industries and do not exceed five per cent in any of the selected industries. There is a slightly higher proportion of administrative and managerial workers than of professional and technical workers, but again this proportion does not exceed five per cent. The proportion of clerical workers range from 3.5 per cent to 20.9 per cent. Production workers form the backbone of the labour force in each of the selected industries. The textile, plywood and particle board, motor vehicle and parts,

Table 5.2 Occupational profile of selected industries for the year 1980

Occupations	Selected Industries										
	Chemical products	Textile	Industrial machinery	Saw milling	Plywood & particle board	Tobacco products	Machinery & parts	Rubber products	Electronics	Motor vehicle & parts	Printing & publishing
Professional & technical	4.5	0.4	2.4	0.2	0.4	0.4	2.1	0.8	0.7	0.6	0.3
Administrative & managerial	5.0	0.9	4.4	1.7	1.2	2.9	3.8	1.1	0.7	1.8	3.2
Clerical	15.6	4.1	13.8	10.5	5.4	3.6	12.7	6.3	3.5	7.6	20.9
Service/sales*	—	0.9	—	—	1.4	0.9	3	0.9	0.4	2.4	2.3*
Production workers:											
Skilled & semi-skilled	30.2	64.8	56.5	48.4	69.5	17.5	59.7	28.7	12.9	67.1	49.9
Unskilled	44.6	28.8	23.0	39.2	22.2	67.2	18.7	62.4	81.9	20.5	22.8

Source: Malaysia *Labour and Manpower Report 1980* Kuala Lumpur: Ministry of Labour, 1981
*denote sales only

machinery and parts and printing and publishing industries have a high proportion (50 per cent to 70 per cent) of skilled and semi-skilled workers. However, the electronics, rubber products, tobacco products and chemical products industries employ a large proportion of unskilled labour. The sawmilling industry has a relatively high proportion, of skilled, semi-skilled and unskilled labour. These figures indicate that there has been a rapid growth in not only the absolute size of the skilled technical workforce, but also in the range of skills required for economic development.

A study by the World Bank, forecasts that Malaysia will require an annual increment of 6 000 technicians and 35 000 skilled workers during the 1980s.[3]

Preliminary detailed projections by the Economic Planning Unit indicate that an additional 690 000 workers will be required in the 1981–85 period, an annual requirement of 138 000 workers, to ensure the economy's rate of progress. The manpower requirements include an annual requirement of 72 000 professional and technical workers, 11 000 administrative and managerial workers, 62 000 clerical workers, 87 000 sales workers, 129 000 service workers and 329 000 production workers.[4]

To ensure a sufficient supply of those categories of manpower in demand, the government has already taken steps to increase and streamline the training facilities of public training institutes, schools and universities. The number of industrial training institutes, polytechnics, technical and vocational schools will be increased and current facilities will be expanded to meet the projected demand. In addition, the course content of such training institutions as well as universities, have been reviewed. In the latter case, the course content has to be modified to be in line with new developments in industry. Local universities are also offering more places for courses that are highly in demand in the country's developing economy. As there are about 180 000 school-leavers each year, with formal education ranging from six to thirteen or more years, and most of whom will enter the job market, there will be no shortage of clerical, sales or production workers. There will also be no lack of administrative and managerial workers as almost 50 per cent of university output are economics and humanities graduates. The supply of professional and technical workers from local training institutes and universities may not be sufficient to meet demand; but graduates in these disciplines returning from foreign universities will help to meet this demand.

Industrial training institutions

The success of Malaysia's export-oriented and resource-base industrialisation hinges to a large extent on the availability of a sufficient pool of skilled manpower; only then would it be possible to ensure the proper utilisation of efficient production methods, stringent quality control techniques and rapid transfer of technology. This, in turn, will enable the domestic industries to produce manufactured goods of high quality which can compete effectively in the world market.

The importance of a ready supply of skilled and semi-skilled manpower has been duly recognised by both the government and private sectors. There are various avenues through which labour is trained within the Malaysian education and educational system (see table 5.3). These include:

1 *Secondary vocational schools* which seek to provide a broad-based education emphasising vocational subjects. The two-year courses in Commerce, Agriculture, Home Science and Engineering Trades, equip less-academically inclined students who have completed their lower secondary education (that is up to Form Three) with the necessary skills for an industrial or factory environment. In 1982, there were a total of 32 vocational schools with an annual output of 6 000 students. Another 13 such schools have been planned, and are expected to commence accepting students by 1985.

Table 5.3 Output from public industrial training institutions for the year 1982

Vocational schools		6 137
Technical schools		2 429
Polytechnics		1 056
Industrial training institutes		
National apprenticeship scheme	87	
Preparatory trade courses	685	
Skill upgrading courses	100	
Hyundai project	257	
Building trade	173	
Instructors training course	91	1 393
Institute Kemahiran Mara		1 728
Youth training centres		
Dusun Tua	612	
Pertak	273	
Kuala Trengganu	83	968
Total		13 711

Source: Malaysia *Labour and Manpower Report 1981/82* Kuala Lumpur: Ministry of Labour, 1984

2 *Secondary technical schools* which form a special branch of the Malaysian school system, and are meant for bright students with an inclination for technical subjects. The technical courses offered in the two-year course are Mechanical Engineering, Civil Engineering, Commerce and Agriculture. The majority of the students proceed on with their tertiary education on completing the course. In 1982, a total of 2 500 students were trained in such technical schools.

3 *Polytechnics* The two polytechnics at present are the Ungku Omar Polytechnic in Ipoh and the Kuantan Polytechnic. Together they trained 1 000 technicians in 1982. The courses offered are mainly Engineering courses, and the Polytechnics' Certificates and Diplomas are recognised by some institutions of higher learning for acceptance into these programmes. Full-time courses are for a period of two years and three months and include a six-months industrial training period.

4 *Industrial training institutes* The Ministry of Labour has set up three such institutes in Kuala Lumpur, Prai (Penang), and Johore Bahru and are completing another two in Kuala Trengganu and Labuan (Sabah). An additional five institutes have been planned and will be located in Ipoh (Perak), Kuantan (Pahang), Malacca, Alor Star (Kedah) and Kota Bahru (Kelantan). The training institutes provide basic industrial skills to unemployed youth and school-leavers. They also provide training courses for upgrading the skills of existing workers. The institutes offer eight types of courses, namely Apprenticeship Courses, Preparatory Trade Courses, Skill Upgrading Courses, Instructional Technique Course, Building Trades, Training in Mechanical, Electrical, Construction and Printing. The courses are geared towards practical training in the workshop, but are balanced with lectures on related theory.

The National Apprenticeship Scheme undertaken by these institutions is a joint effort by the government and industry to meet the requirements for skilled workers. While the government provides free training facilities, employers sponsor apprentices of their choice and provide in-plant training facilities for them. At another level, the Centre for Instructor and Advanced Skill Training (CIAST) has been established and will be operational in 1985. Its purpose is to upgrade the skills of instructors and supervisors in vocational training institutions, and to provide advanced skill training to skilled workers. The courses are short, being of three to ten weeks in duration.

The National Industrial Training and Trade Certification Board (NITTCB) is a body which oversees the training of industrial skills in both the public and private sectors. It reviews training content, sets trade standards and conducts trade certification exercises in colloboration with the private sector. It has set National Trade Standards for 29 trades. The purpose of the Board is to ensure that labour trained in both private and public skill-training institutions, conform to the requirements of industry. In 1982, a total of about 12 000 candidates were tested at Basic Grade level, 2 600 at Intermediate Grade level and 80 were tested at Advanced Grade level. Out of these only about 50 per cent were awarded the NITTCB Certificates.

5 *Institute Kemahiran Mara* These institutes have been established under the Ministry of National Development with the aim of providing institutional and on-the-job training facilities for Bumiputra workers. There are altogether nine training centres, with plans for another four to be built during the 1981–85 period. The courses offered emphasise industrial and commercial trades.

6 *Youth training centres* There are at present three such centres and they are administered by the Ministry of Culture, Youth and Sports. They provide the trainees with work discipline as well as vocational and commercial skills.

7 *Private sector training* Apart from the efforts made by the government, industrial training is also provided by private sector. Private sector training institutes are generally profit-making ventures; nevertheless, they contribute greatly to the provision of skilled manpower for the economy. While their forté is still in commercial training such as accountancy, secretarial studies and data processing, several have ventured into industrial training, particularly in electrical, mechanical and printing trades. An example is the Federal Institute of Technology in Petaling Jaya which prepares students for the London City and Guilds Examinations.

Trade unions have also become involved in industrial training and two such establishments are The Workers' Institute of Technology and the Agro-Industrial Training Centre. In 1982, the total output from the 15 largest private-sector training institutes is 2 100 trainees.

The industrial sector itself has collaborated with the public sector to increase the supply of skilled labour. Besides providing in-plant and on-site facilities to trainees from the public industrial training institutes, several establishments have also their own in-plant training schemes.

Institutes of higher learning

There is a great demand for tertiary education in Malaysia. Many Malaysians aspire towards a university education and a degree is highly valued in Malaysian society; it also enhances the employment prospects of the holder and more often than not is the passport to a well-paid job. The government has recognised this need and has established five universities to fulfil the demand: the University of Malaya (UM), National University of Malaysia (UKM), Science University of Malaysia (USM), Agricultural University of Malaysia (UPM) and the University of Technology Malaysia (UTM). Another two universities have also been established recently: the International Islamic University and the Northern University of Malaysia (UUM).

In addition, there are two colleges, the Mara Institute of Technology (ITM) and the Tunku Abdul Rahman College (TAR) which offer diploma and certificate courses as well as some external degree courses. They produce manpower at the sub-professional and technical level. Together, these institutes of higher learning provide the bulk of necessary professional, technical and management personnel needed by local industries.

The *University of Malaya (UM)* was the first university to be established in Malaysia and is located in Kuala Lumpur. As can be seen from table 5.4, it has the highest output among the five universities; about 39 per cent of the total number of basic degree graduates and the largest number of postgraduate students. It has the largest science and engineering faculties among the local universities.

The *National University of Malaysia (UKM)* in Bangi, Selangor has been earmarked by the government to be the main university in Malaysia. Its output has been increasing sharply compared to a slight decline in UM. The university is also placing more emphasis on its science faculty and its output of Science graduates have more than doubled between 1978 and 1982. However, its strength still lies mainly in the Humanities and Social Sciences.

The *Science University of Malaya (USM)* is located in Penang and has a smaller output compared to UM and UKM. In 1982, 53 per cent of its output were graduates in Science, Educational Science, Applied Science, Pharmacy and Housing Building and Planning.

The *University of Technology Malaysia (UTM)* contributes mainly to the technical and professional manpower needs of the country. Its degree courses are all technical in nature and it does not cater for the Arts and Social Sciences. It also offers a large number of technical courses at the diploma level.

The *Agricultural University (UPM)* is concerned mainly with the supply of high level agro-based manpower as indicated in table 5.4. It was established in 1971 at Serdang (Selangor) and courses are offered in Agriculture, Forestry, Agribusiness, Veterinary Medicine and Animal Science. It offers courses at both the degree and diploma level.

In table 5.5, we have presented the official estimates of the output of skilled and semi-skilled manpower from public training institu-

Table 5.4 Output from local universities

	1978	1979	1980	1981	1982
University Malaya					
Post Degree:	77	74	80	76	57
Degree: Economics/Accounting/Arts	991	1 035	1 082	985	1 065
Law	54	50	47	54	85
Science/Educational Science	327	436	502	356	394
Engineering	209	175	156	138	135
Medicine	119	125	101	134	110
Dentistry	30	31	32	29	27
Diploma: Education	680	667	596	521	486
Business Admin./Accounting/Public Admin.	50	42	23	46	36
Computer Science	1	7	—	12	19
Interpretation/Translation/Teaching English Language	62	65	54	56	73
Subtotal:	2 600	2 707	2 673	2 407	2 437
National University of Malaysia					
Post Degree:	3	4	9	8	9
Degree: Economics (G.D.)/Humanities and Social Science	422	376	398	116	846
Islamic Studies/Malay Language, Culture and Literature Am	225	238	174	210	356
Science	130	190	113	258	300
Medicine	—	37	37	55	104
Diploma: Education	—	—	275	340	122
Islamic Studies/Islamic Studies (certificate)	—	—	10	28	—
Subtotal:	781	845	1 016	1 015	1 737
Science University (USM)					
Post Degree:	26	24	15	2	1
Degree: Science/Science with Education/Applied Science	250	166	215	216	320
Pharmacy	39	36	49	48	46
Housing, Building and Planning	33	41	51	36	42
Social Science/Humanities/Humanities and Education	412	386	364	62	355
Subtotal:	760	653	694	364	764

Table 5.4 (cont.)

	1978	1979	1980	1981	1982
University of Technology Malaysia (UTM)					
Degree: Civil, Mechanical, Petroleum, Electrical Engineering	59	55	81	79	88
Land Surveying/Quantity Surveying	21	21	35	28	33
Architecture	3	8	13	6	11
Property Management/Town and Regional Development	17	19	35	42	44
Diploma: Civil, Mechanical, Petroleum, Electrical (Power), Electrical Engineering	329	332	311	393	429
Land Surveying/Quantity Surveying	60	76	63	101	110
Architecture	34	33	35	43	73
Property Management/Town and Regional Development	19	55	62	68	78
Science with Education	63	47	84	127	155
Subtotal:	605	646	719	887	1 021
Agricultural University					
Post Degree:	1	1	2	5	13
Degree: Science (with Education)	—	34	56	25	27
Environment	—	—	11	9	7
Economic/Agribusiness	87	83	74	119	102
Veterinary Surgeons	14	22	18	12	20
Forestry	20	28	21	19	11
Agriculture/Agricultural Engineering, Education	89	107	88	136	153
Food Technology Science/Home Science Technology	—	—	25	35	28
Diploma: Agriculture/Animal Health and Production Husbandry	328	242	246	218	181
Home Science Technology	28	22	21	—	—
Fishery/Forestry	25	55	41	35	30
Science with Education	133	178	190	193	167
Subtotal:	725	772	793	806	739

Source: Malaysia, Labour and Manpower Report 1981/82 Kuala Lumpur: Ministry of Labour, 1984

Table 5.5 Malaysia: enrolment and output of skilled and semi-skilled manpower from public training institutions, 1981–85[1]

Institution	Enrolment		Output			Total output 1981–85
	1980	1985	1981	1983	1985	
Vocational schools	12 595	21 054	6 589	7 922	9 871	40 385
Technical schools	5 220	6 520	2 836	3 150	3 220	15 256
Youth training centres	1 331	1 617	1 057	1 217	1 217	5 761
Agricultural institutes	1 188	1 532	465	447	596	2 402
Industrial Training Institutes	1 538	3 540	940	1 010	1 620	5 845
Institiut Kemahiran MARA	2 871	6 704	2 209	2 240	4 020	13 081
Institiut Perdagangan MARA	270	1 850	200	540	1 660	3 740
Kolej Tunku Abdul Rahman	451	1 945	230	506	811	2 533
Politeknik Ungku Omar	1 551	1 744	638	742	752	3 611
Politeknik Kuantan	575	1 330	213	330	594	1 929
Total	27 590	47 836	15 377	18 104	24 361	94 543

Source: Malaysia *Fourth Malaysia Plan 1981–85* Kuala Lumpur: Government Printer, 1981

Note: [1]This is the certificate-level manpower and the courses provided at these institutions include various engineering trades, building trades, printing trades as well as courses in commerce, Agricultural Science, Home Science and other related courses. The data include enrolment and output from skill-upgrading courses undertaken by industrial training institutes and Institiut Kemahiran MARA

tions. In 1983, about 18 000 skilled and semi-skilled workers will be trained. To 1985, the skilled manpower output from polytechnics, TAR college and MARA training institutes will be about 3 300, while that from industrial and agricultural institutes will be about 1 400. Vocational schools, technical schools and youth training centres will produce the largest number (11 200) of semi-skilled manpower. Overall output is also projected to increase at an increasing rate (14 per cent to 17 per cent) during the 1982–85 period. The figures suggest that the output from training institutions will be sufficient for the country's skilled and semi-skilled manpower needs.

Analysis of output at the course level from public training institutes show that about 89 000 people will be trained in various trades such as engineering, building, printing, commerce, agriculture, home science, skill-upgrading courses and others, during the period 1981–85. Skilled and semi-skilled output from the engineering and building trades will be the most in demand. The largest output, numbering about 44 000 is from the engineering trades, followed by an output of 15 000 from the building trades during the same period. The figures indicate that scarcity of skilled labour which in turn will hamper industrial growth, may be overcome in the 1980s.

Supply of skilled and professional manpower

The five major universities (UM, UKM, USM, UPM and UTM) and the two colleges (ITM and TAR) had an output of 8 533 students and 9 631 degree and diploma graduates in 1981 and 1982 respectively. The figures indicate a very significant increase of 12.9 per cent in output during the two-year period. However, the increment in output is expected to decline after 1983. During the period 1981–85, a total of 53 056 students will graduate from local universities and colleges. In addition, there are at least 52 000 Malaysian students in foreign institutions of higher learning at any time and the figure may increase further, the number of students enrolled overseas increased from about 40 000 in 1980 to about 58 000 in 1983. Of the total number of students in 1983, about 35 300 (60.8 per cent) pursuing courses at degree level; 6 860 (11.8 per cent) at diploma level; 7 520 (12.9 per cent) at certificate level and 8 300 (14.3 per cent) in secondary level education. The USA, Britain, Canada and India were hosts to the largest number of Malaysian students.

Trade unionism in Malaysia

Under the Trade Union Ordinance of 1959, a trade union in Malaysia is any association or combination of workmen or employees, within any particular or similar trade, occupation or industry. The purposes of forming trade unions are to regulate relations between workers and management, to represent either workers or management in trade disputes and (when the need arises) to organise industrial action and to provide financial support to members during a strike or lock-out.

In addition, to the 1959 Trade Union Ordinance, there are two other important instruments that regulate the relationship between employers and workers in Malaysia: the 1967 Industrial Relations Act, the 1955 Employment Ordinance. The Industrial Relations Act is an important instrument which set up the procedure governing the formalised relations between employers and workers and their trade unions. The Employment Ordinance, explained in greater detail in chapter 7, deals with the terms and conditions of work once a contract of service is signed between the employer and the employee. While trade unions in Malaysia have to be registered to be recognised, there is no restriction on the establishment of legally constituted unions. There are three categories of trade unions that are allowed under the Trade Union Ordinance: employees' trade unions; employers' trade unions and federation of trade unions. In 1973, there were 340 trade unions and its growth fluctuated with the economic performance of the country. By 1982, the number of trade unions had increased to 383 with a total membership of about 610 000, representing 17 per cent of the total Malaysian wage earners.

There are three federations of trade unions: Congress of Unions of Employees in the Public and Civil Service (CUEPACS), Kongress Kesatuan Guru-Guru dalam Perkhidmatan Pelajaran (KKGPP) and Sarawak Wharf Labourers' Union Federation. The former two federations are in the public sector while the latter is in the private sector. CUEPACS is the largest federation of trade unions, 57 (or 41 per cent) of the unions in the public sector are affiliated to it. The KKGPP has 3 (out of 28) teachers' unions as affiliates and its membership is 25 per cent of the total membership in the educational services. The Sarawak Wharf Labourers' Union Federation is an affiliation of 14 Wharf Labourers' Unions.

At the apex of the trade union movement are the Malaysian Trade Unions Congress (MTUC) and the Malaysian Federation of Employers (MEF) which are the spokesmen for workers and employers, respectively. They are both registered as societies under the Societies Act; and the membership of both organisations is open to all industries. The MTUC in particular, is a force to be reckoned within the Malaysian trade union movement; in 1982, its affiliates numbered 102.

On the whole, Malaysian trade unions are small in terms of membership. In 1982, the membership of 50 per cent of the 272 employees' unions was below 500; 40 per cent had a membership of between 500 and 5 000 members and only 10 per cent had a membership strength exceeding 5 000 members. Union membership is predominantly male; female members formed only a quarter of the 530 000 members in Peninsular Malaysia in 1982. The racial distribution of union membership is about 51 per cent Malays, 25 per cent Indians and 22 per cent Chinese in Peninsular Malaysia.

Out of a total of 362 trade unions in Malaysia, 109 or 47 per cent are house unions and their membership amount to 25 per cent of the total union membership of 610 000. Within the private sector, 36 (or 24 per cent) of the 148 unions are house unions with a membership of 6 per cent of the total union membership of 310 000 in the private sector.

An analysis of the rate of unionisation (see table 5.6) reveals that the service sector is the most heavily unionised, having 149 of the total of 274 unions in 1982 for Peninsular Malaysia and a membership of about 38 per cent of the total membership. This is followed by the manufacturing, and transport and storage sectors with 47 and 31 unions, respectively. However, the membership of these two sectors is less than that of the agriculture sector which, with only 19 unions, has about 24 per cent of the total membership.

The Malaysian industrial climate has been relatively peaceful since the mid-1970s. The number of strikes have declined from 64 in 1975 to 26 in 1982 (see table 5.7), followed by a corresponding decline in the percentage of total union membership involved in these strikes, from 2.5 per cent to 0.6 per cent, respectively. The substantially higher number of strikes during the 1975–76 period was chiefly triggered by the inflationary pressures which prevailed at that time. In addition, the number of man-days lost during industrial strikes have decreased appreciably; from 20 000 man-days in 1980 to 10 000 man-days in 1982, as the disputes which led to the strikes were more quickly resolved.

Recruitment procedures

Unskilled labour

Recruitment of unskilled labour, unlike that of skilled labour, does not encounter problems of scarcity in supply. In fact, each year there are about 180 000 school leavers who enter the job market for the first time and form a large pool of unskilled labour from which employers can select their intake. Many of them have sat for public examinations such as the Lower Certificate of Examination (involving 9 years of schooling), or the Malaysian Certificate of Examination (requiring 11 years of schooling) or the Higher School Certificate Examination.

Table 5.6 Structure and size of trade unions co-related with industrial grouping Peninsular Malaysia (1977–82)

Industrial grouping	No. of unions			Membership		
	1977	1980	1982	1977	1980	1982
Agriculture	18	20	19	142 723	138 449	135 739
Mining	4	4	4	9 700	8 401	8 327
Manufacturing	42	48	47	68 703	87 320	92 80[illegible]
Construction	3	4	4	1 762	1 204	1 950
Electricity, gas and water	6	6	6	12 190	14 676	17 025
Commerce	13	14	14	30 740	36 181	41 597
Transport and storage	27	28	31	49 568	48 229	54 908
Service	152	152	149	137 881	197 280	212 327
Total	265	276	274	503 267	531 740	564 674

Source: Ministry of Labour
Note: This table includes employers' trade unions and shows membership on Register

Table 5.7 Strikes and union membership involved

Year	No. of strikes	No. of workers involved	Total unions membership*	Percentage of membership involved
1975	64	12 124	477 565	2.5
1976	70	20 040	481 736	4.2
1977	40	7 783	503 267	1.6
1978	36	6 792	523 620	1.3
1979	28	5 629	520 024	1.1
1980	28	3 402	531 740	0.6
1981	24	4 832	548 434	0.9
1982	26	3 330	564 674	0.6

Source: Ministry of Labour
*Membership on Register excluding employers' unions

The most common means of employing unskilled production workers is to post a notice on the factory gate inviting applications from those who are interested and suitably qualified. This method has the advantage of employing workers who live in the vicinity of the factory and management does not face the problem of arranging for their accommodation and transportation. Unskilled labour can be recruited by advertising in the nationally circulated newspaper or regional newspapers. Such advertisements normally inform the public of walk-in interviews or open interviews scheduled at convenient locations. These interviews seldom require correspondence as candidates present themselves at the stated place and time to meet with the interviewers.

Another method that is frequently used for the recruitment of unskilled labour is through employment agencies. The Public Employment Service in Malaysia performs the function of a clearing house by matching job openings reported by employers with the attributes of registrants. It is a government agency and has 35 offices in Peninsular Malaysia and eight each in Sabah and Sarawak. Job applicants register themselves with the agencies by giving their personal details, training, work experience and job category preference.

Skilled labour

As in any country that is rapidly industrialising, scarcity of skilled labour poses a problem. While employment growth slackened in almost all sectors of the Malaysian economy in the past few years, the labour market situation tightened in the expanding construction industry and in the less attractive agricultural sector. Within the manufacturing sector there is a skilled labour shortage in the following sectors: (i) weavers and related workers (ii) cabinet-makers and related workers (iii) machinery fitters, assemblers and repairers (iv) machine tool operators (v) electrical wiremen (vi) bookbinders and related workers (vii) carpenters, joiners and parquetry workers and (viii) labourers not elsewhere classified.

The shortage of skilled labour is due to a variety of reasons, among them are competition from Singapore, the attitudes of workers to blue-collar jobs and the inability of training institutions to meet the increased needs (in terms of quantum and types and levels of skills required) in the affected sectors.

Although it is difficult for Malaysia to compete with Singapore in terms of better wages the other problems can be overcome. It is true that most Malaysians have a preference for white-collar jobs but the attitude towards blue-collar jobs is changing. A study conducted by SERU (or the socio-economic research unit of the Prime Minister's Department) indicated that many job-seekers, youths and parents have a positive attitude towards blue-collar jobs in terms of their income earning capacity, the job security and the status attributed to such jobs. Training institutions have increased their existing facilities and expanded their programmes to train more youths for occupations of high demand.

The most effective means of recruiting skilled labour are through employment agencies and advertisements in newspapers. Besides public employment agencies, there are also private employment agencies which have mushroomed througout the country. These private agencies are regulated by the 1980 Employment Agencies Act. Advertisements in nationally circulated dailies usually call attention to walk-in interviews conducted at various convenient locations.

Participation by industry in the training schemes of industrial training institutes is another good way to recruit potential skilled workers. During the in-plant training phase of their courses, trainees will be introduced to the working environment and may be sufficiently attracted to stay. Employees can also sponsor trainees at such training institutes.

Clerical

Clerical and related jobs are white-collar jobs which many Malaysians with educational achievement up to the School Certificate or Higher School Certificate levels aspire. This group of occupations range from simple clerical duties to bookkeeping and simple accounting to stenographic and secretarial duties. The basic requirements are the ability to read and write, but many job-seekers further equip themselves with bookkeeping, typing and other secretarial skills. There is a multitude of private commercial institutions offering courses in typing, shorthand, secretarial duties, bookkeeping and data processing. Many students in these private institutions take qualifying examinations which are conducted by well-known British institutions. In addition, the Malaysian school syllabus also includes subjects such as Principles of Accounts and Commerce in the upper secondary school.

Recruitment of clerical staff is most often conducted through classified advertisements in newspapers stating employers' requirements and inviting interested parties to write or call personally. Depending on the size of the firm, recruitment can be fast and simple for the smaller firms, while larger establishments prefer a wider and more thorough screening process. Employment agencies are also good avenues for recruitment of clerical workers. In 1982, the Public Employment Service placed about 5 000 clerical workers against vacancies notified totaling about 8 000 jobs. Another 38 000 registrants at the Public Employment Service were unplaced for this job category. There is an oversupply of this category of workers.

Professional and managerial

The professional category of workers include those with a university degree or those who have graduated from colleges, commercial institutions or polytechnics. The latter group can be further subclassified as semi-professionals. Many of the professionals have graduated with degrees in Economics, Business Administration, Natural and Applied Sciences as well as the Humanities and Social Sciences. During the period 1981–90, about 35 000 Arts graduates (Arts, Humanities, Economics and Business), 31 000 Science graduates (Medicine, Dentistry, Agriculture and related Sciences) and 7 600 technical graduates will enter the job market after completing degree courses at local universities. Their ranks will be further increased by Malaysian students graduating from foreign universities. At the diploma level, there will be 21 700 Arts graduates, 5 300 Science graduates and 14 500 technical graduates will join the labour market during the same period 1981–90.

The most common form of recruitment for staff at the professional and managerial level is advertisement in newspapers. Relevant information on the desired qualifications and the job specifications and the company are included in the advertisements to permit some degree of self-screening on the part of potential applicants. Response is usually good and in highly sought after sectors, overwhelming. The search for a particularly qualified personnel or top level professional is often conducted through an intermediary such as a consulting firm.

There are several such 'head hunting' organisations in Malaysia; and the consulting firm will conduct the search either through advertising in local newspapers or through personal contacts. Another alternative is the Professional Employment Bureau which caters for both fresh graduates and those who are seeking enhanced job openings. The Bureau registers only those with degrees/diplomas from local/ overseas universities and colleges.

Employment and the New Economic Policy

In line with the guidelines set by the NEP, the employment policies of firms in various sectors of the economy and at all levels should reflect the overall composition of the population, particularly in areas where Bumiputras are seriously under-represented such as in middle and upper management levels.

To ensure the success of the NEP, the government has implemented various policy measures and set into motion several programmes. It is redesigning education and training programmes to increase the supply of trained Bumiputras manpower. It has provided direct incentives and taken administrative measures to accelerate the participation of Bumiputras in the modern sectors of the economy; that is the secondary and tertiary sectors of the economy. In line with these developments, significant changes in the ethnic composition of the workforce have been observed in the last decade. The proportion of Malays in the service sector has increased from 39 per cent to 51 per cent while that of the industrial sector has increased from 31 per cent to 39 per cent, during the period 1970–80. A corresponding decrease has occurred among non-Malays most notably among the Chinese category. The proportion of Indians has increased in the industrial sector but decreased in the service sector over the same period reported. However, it must be emphasised that the absolute number of employees of all ethnic groups in each sector has increased as the restructuring took place within an expanding economy.

The government has also stepped up efforts to train Malay executives for management and technical levels. The ethnic structure on individual occupational groups in table 5.8 reflects the effect of the NEP on employment practices. An increase in the proportion of Malays has been recorded for all occupational groups during the past decade 1970–80. In the professional, technical and related workers occupational group, the proportion of Malays increased significantly from 46 per cent to 55 per cent during the period under study while that of the administrative and managerial workers category has increased moderately from 36 per cent to 50 per cent. An examination of the racial composition of eight professions with affiliated

Table 5.8 Percentage distribution of experienced labour force aged 10 and over by occupational group and ethnic group, Peninsular Malaysia, 1970 and 1980

Occupational group	Number (thousands)		*Malays*		*Chinese*		*Indians*		*Others*	
	1970	1980	1970	1980	1970	1980	1970	1980	1970	1980
Professional, technical and related workers	129.4	261.9	46	55	39	34	13	10	3	1
Administrative and managerial workers	30.3	38.2	23	26	65	64	8	6	4	4
Clerical and related workers	133.3	304.5	36	50	48	39	15	10	1	1
Sales workers	236.7	357.3	23	29	66	63	11	8	—	—
Service workers	225.4	331.2	46	59	39	29	13	12	2	1
Agricultural, animal husbandry and forestry workers, fishermen and hunters	1 322.1	1 256.3	69	70	21	18	9	11	1	1
Production and related workers, transport equipment operators and labourers	542.8	993.5	34	42	55	46	11	12	—	—
Occupation not adequately described or not stated	126.3	250.2	56	54	33	35	10	10	1	1
Total	2 736.4	3 793.1	52	54	36	35	10	11	1	1

Source: General Report of Population Census, 1980

professional bodies such as accountants and architects over the period 1980–82, reveals that the proportion of Malays has increased moderately while that of the Chinese has remained stable.[5]

To date, the NEP has been fairly successful with regard to its employment policies. While the various sectors of the economy are ready to comply with government guidelines, it is the scarcity in supply of Bumiputra manpower to the relevant sectors and levels of job hierarchy which could hamper their smooth implementation. But this contingency has been anticipated, and the numerous programmes have been implemented by the government to rectify the problem. Private enterprises have also started their own training programmes to meet the quotas placed on the racial composition of their employees.

6

Marketing system

The Malaysian business market is both complex and diverse. This is particularly true of the market for consumer products. For a relatively small population of 14.1 m., the number of sub-markets or segments that can be distinguished is very large. This multiplicity in market segmentation is due to the multi-ethnic background, as well as the widely differing income and educational levels of the Malaysian population.

The multi-ethnic composition of the Malaysian population is differentiated further by differences in cultural practices, languages and dialects as well as religion. For example, the Malays constitute the largest ethnic group (55 per cent) of the population in Peninsular Malaysia. They are Muslims and speak Bahasa Malaysia which is the national language of the country. The Chinese, mostly third or fourth generation descendants of their forefathers who migrated from China, are the next largest group, representing 34 per cent of the population. Their religion and culture are based on an amalgamation of Confucianism, Taoism and Buddhism. They speak a variety of dialects, the most important of which are Hokkien, Cantonese and Khek (Hakka). In addition, Mandarin is used as the medium of instruction in Chinese vernacular schools. The Indians are the third major ethnic group (10 per cent) in Malaysia. They are mostly Hindus and, to a limited extent, Christians. Most of them are descendants of early emigrants from the Indian sub-continent who came to work on the rubber estates during the colonial days. In addition to these three ethnic groups, there are the natives of Sarawak and Sabah such as the Ibans, Kadazans, Bidayuhs and the *Orang Asli* of Peninsular Malaysia.

Age-wise, the Malaysian labour market is 'youthful'; 34 per cent of the population is below 25 years of age, comprising mainly juveniles, young single working adults and young married couples. The 25–39 age group constitutes more than one-third (38 per cent) of the labour force. Its members are mainly young married couples with dependant children. The 40–59 age group represents about 25 per cent of the population while the 60 and above age group constitutes only about 3 per cent of the population.[1]

With the expansion of educational opportunities, the number of persons attending educational institutions in Malaysia has increased by 39 per cent to 3.2 m. persons during the decade of 1970–80. By 1980, virtually all Malaysians between the ages of 10 to 20 have attended school and can be considered literate. Little disparity could be discerned between the proportion of young males and females who receive education but for those above 40 years of age the male literacy rate is markedly higher than that for the females. Using the ability to read newspapers and letters or to write letters as a measure, 72 per cent of the Malaysian population 10 years and above are literate while a further 3 per cent are semi-literate. Literacy in Bahasa Malaysia and English stand at 75 per cent and 30 per cent respectively for the population aged 10 and above. Taking into consideration the fact that education is universally available and free the literacy rate is expected to improve further in the years to come.

The Malaysian distribution system

The wholesale and retail sector has contributed significantly to the Malaysian gross domestic product (GDP). While its absolute contribution has fluctuated in recent years, its percentage contribution to the GDP has been quite consistent; from 12.8 per cent in 1973 to 13.5 per cent in 1982 (see table 6.1).

The highly heterogeneous nature of the Malaysian market is compounded by the 'small-unit' purchase pattern which in turn can be attributed to a relatively low purchasing power. The nature of the market has, therefore, created the need for a distribution system that is long and intensive.

The distribution system in Malaysia can be viewed as a pyramid with very few but large agency houses and major wholesalers at the apex. They are linked by smaller distributors, wholesalers and other middle-men down to the shopkeepers or traders who retail the goods in towns and villages to the people. The scale of operation decreases while the number of establishments increases towards the base of the distribution pyramid. The agency houses are often the importers for many foreign-brand goods as they hold the franchises for many foreign consumer and industrial products. In the case of locally manufactured goods, major wholesalers market the goods to other intermediaries or secondary wholesalers in the channel. The secondary wholesalers, in turn, perform further bulk-breaking functions to supply a multiplicity of retailers who are sufficiently widespread and

Table 6.1 Contribution of wholesale and retail trade to total gross domestic product (GDP)

Year	Total GDP $Mm.[1]	% Contribution of		
		Wholesale & retail[2]	Manufacturing	Agriculture[3]
1973	15 904	12.8	15.8	29.1
1974	17 227	12.8	16.1	28.8
1975	17 365	12.8	16.4	27.7
1976	19 373	12.4	17.4	27.8
1977	20 875	12.4	17.9	26.4
1978	22 264	12.7	18.3	25.2
1979	24 324	13.0	18.4	24.9
1980	26 228	13.5	18.6	23.8
1981	28 092	13.4	18.2	23.2
1982	29 553	13.5	17.9	23.4
1983[4]	31 206[4]	13.4[4]	18.2[4]	22.6[4]

Source: Malaysia *Economic Reports*, Ministry of Finance, various years
Notes: 1 In 1970 constant prices
2 Includes hotels and restaurants
3 Includes livestock, forestry and fishery
4 Estimates by MIAPE (Macro Inter-Agency Planning Group)

small in operation, to sell goods in small quantities to a dispersed market. In many instances, it is the credit mechanism which holds the pyramid together. Within the pyramid, the agency houses are the chief suppliers of credit. However, many of the larger intermediaries also obtain their financing from banks while the smaller intermediaries usually have to depend on their personal resources or may resort to money-lenders (*chettiars*) for financing.

A new form of marketing which is gaining widespread popularity with Malaysian consumers is 'direct selling'. In this marketing system, the importers or local manufacturers employ individuals to sell 'direct' to friends and acquaintances within the homes. To date, direct selling has been limited to household products, toiletries and apparels. The success of this system is based on the ability of its 'distributors' to recruit other distributors from friends, relatives and customers. An intricate system of mark-ups, discounts and bonuses are employed to motivate distributors who may work on a part-time or full-time basis.

In industrial marketing, transactions are direct between the manufacturer and the user; or the two parties may be linked by a minimal number of intermediaries, known as dealers, who may either hold the franchise to the product or are alloted prespecified areas as their sales territory. This is particularly true for technically complicated imported goods, such as machinery and precision equipment, which are marketed through specialist distributors who have been trained and are in the position to provide the necessary services.

With respect to the structure of the wholesale and the retail trade there were about 17 900 wholesale and 90 000 retail establishments in Peninsular Malaysia in 1980, compared to 12 200 and 72 500 in 1974 respectively (see table 6.2). During the six-year period, the value of output from wholesale establishments has doubled ($M14.6 billion in 1974 to $M29.2 billion) while that of retail establishments has more than doubled (from $M5.0 billion in 1974 to $M12.1 billion). The figures for urban areas in Peninsular Malaysia, show an even greater increase in the output values; a 118 per cent increase in the output value of wholesale establishments and a 179 per cent increase for output value of retail establishments over the period 1974–80. The figures indicate that the distribution network in the urban areas of Peninsular Malaysia has expanded more rapidly than that for the country as a whole.

With reference to the number of establishments in 1980, 13 300 of the total 17 900 wholesale establishments in Peninsular Malaysia were in the urban areas; these urban wholesale outlets accounted for 66.6 per cent of the value of output. Thus wholesale establishments are mainly located in the large urban centres, and they (urban wholesale outlets) control a greater part of the wholesale business. This is consistent with the fact that the urban areas are commercial centres which have the necessary infrastructural supporting services for the operation of efficient wholesalers. However, only 14.8 per cent of the 90 000 retail establishments are in the urban centres, but they account for 65.5 per cent of the total retail output value of $M12 107 m. in 1980. This indicates that retail outlets in the urban areas are generally large outlets. The largest store and retail chains are all in the urban areas where the inhabitants of the more densely populated urban areas are more affluent, and generally prefer to shop in the more comfortable environment offered by large retailers in outlets such as supermarkets or convenient stores.

Having briefly discussed the nature of the Malaysian wholesale and retail sector, I will elaborate in greater detail the structure of each of these two sectors.

Major importers and agency houses

The wholesale trade is the resale (without transformation) of new and used goods to retailers, industrial, commercial, institutional or professional users, or to other wholesalers, acting as agents in buying

Table 6.2 Wholesale and retail outlets in Peninsular Malaysia

Year	Wholesale				Retail			
	Peninsular Malaysia		Urban areas		Peninsular Malaysia		Urban areas	
	No. of establishments	Value of output ($Mm.)	No. of establishments	Value of output ($Mm.)	No. of establishments	Value of output ($Mm.)	No. of establishments	Value of output ($Mm.)
1974	12 202	14 577	9 185	12 523	72 505	5 001	6 990	2 836
1976	13 230	16 305	9 961	15 087	80 175	6 564	8 318	3 620
1978	15 121	21 344	11 404	19 475	74 838	7 924	10 128	5 154
1980	17 907	29 235	13 287	27 266	90 037	12 107	13 334	7 925

Source: Malaysia *Sample Survey of Wholesale and Retail Trades in Peninsular Malaysia/Urban Areas* Department of Statistics, various years

merchandise for persons or companies. Wholesale institutions include import-export agents and merchants, distributors and dealers. In Malaysia, the merchants and agents are responsible for handling nearly all the imports and exports of the country. Among the agents, the agency houses are the most important. They hold exclusive rights and agencies to many of the major imports. Some of the large agency houses in Malaysia include Hagemeyer (which holds the agencies for popular household consumer durable brand names such as JVC, KDK and Olympia), Eastern Agency (for a large range of liqueur), Guthrie (now renamed Mulpha), Boustead, Sime Darby, Harrison and Grossfield among others.

The dozen or so agency houses originated during the colonial days and they are still the most important institutions to have ownership and control of the Malaysian distribution system.[2] Besides possessing the franchise for the import of many well-known brand goods, they are also active participants in the Malaysian economy. They hold shipping and insurance agencies (especially cargo insurance) and are active in manufacturing, tin-mining and banking.

Agency houses may be divided into three groups. Firstly, they may specialise in imports or exports by acting as selling agents for foreign manufacturers and as purchasing agents for manufacturers' representatives. Secondly, they may specialise in managing enterprises, belonging to foreign investors. Thirdly, they may combine some or all the above activities.

While the agency houses and merchants form the top echelon of the wholesale distributive system, there are other wholesale institutions such as distributors, dealers, small-scale wholesalers and wholesale commission agents who serve as secondary wholesalers and link the agency houses and other large importers to the myriad of retailers who form the bottom echelon of the distributive pyramid. In addition, the wholesalers also act as distributors for locally manufactured products. The manufacturers' distributors, importers and agency houses are large in size and operate in the larger towns. In contrast, smaller dealers and wholesalers, who serve as links further down the channel, are found in the smaller towns and villages.

In addition, there are government agencies such as Pernas, which participate in the import-export trade; in fact, Pernas, is the sole agent responsible for the Malaysia-China trade. There are also fledgling trading houses or *sogososhas*[3] in Malaysia, such as the Malaysian Overseas Investment Corporation (MOIC), Sime Darby-Pernas Trading Corporation, Multi-Purpose International Trading Corporation, Malaysian International Trading Corporation (MITCO) and Malaysian Trans-National Trading (MATRA) Corporation Bhd which at present function as trading companies but were incorporated with the intention of managing more effectively the marketing of Malaysian imports and exports.

The wholesale organisations operate on a variety of mark-ups and discounts. The margins differ between products and between different levels of distributors. On the whole, Malaysian wholesale establishments have not been very aggressive in their operations. They rarely use innovative promotional methods to improve demand through the channel and are contented with the usual trade discounts to maintain channel relationships. There is a lack of concerted efforts on the part of the wholesalers to improve services to other members in the distribution channel. The services provided are basically bulk-breaking and provision of trade credit to other members in the channel.

In 1980, there were a total of 17 900 wholesale establishments in Peninsular Malaysia (see table 6.3). Of these only 4 900 (27.8 per cent) recorded on annual output of more than $M1.0 m. Only 5.1 per cent of the establishments were really large and had an annual turnover exceeding $M5.0 m., however, this 5.1 per cent of the wholesale establishments accounted for 56.4 per cent of the total value of output of all wholesale establishments in Peninsular Malaysia. The majority of the larger wholesale establishments (annual turnover exceeding $M1.0 m.) are in the urban areas. In 1980, all wholesale establishments with an annual turnover exceeding $M5.0 m. were in the urban areas. With regard to employment size, in 1980, 95 per cent of the wholesale establishments employed less than 20 people while 83.3 per cent of the establishments employed less than 10 people. All wholesale establishments which employ more than 50 people are located in the urban commercial centres[4] (see table 6.4).

The wholesale sector consists of a number of subsectors. From table 6.5, it can be seen that the wholesaling of food items was valued at about $M5.9 billion (out of a total output value of $M29.2 billion) in 1980 and is characterised by a large number (4 225) of establishments involved. The output from the apparel (clothing, textile and footwear) subsector was valued at $M1.2 billion with 883 wholesalers.

The wholesale business of transport vehicles and parts (including bicycles, motor vehicles, motor-cycles and parts), was valued at $M2.9 billion from 2 524 establishments. For the petrol wholesaling business, a total of $M3.7 billion worth of petrol was distributed by 324 wholesale establishments, while the lumber and building materials sector had an output of $M4.5 billion with 3 663 distributors involved. These figures indicate clearly the highly heterogeneous nature of the Malaysian wholesale business.

Retailers and retailing outlets

The retail trade is defined as the resale (without transformation) of new and used goods to the general public, for personal or household

Table 6.3 Wholesale establishments by output size, Peninsular Malaysia

Output size group ($M thousand)	No. of establishments			Value of output ($Mm.)		
	1974	1978	1980	1974	1978	1980
Peninsular Malaysia: <50	1 718	1 797	1 542	40	43	43
50–249	3 650	3 917	4 985	503	524	667
250–999	3 858	5 407	6 398	2 016	2 885	3 499
1 000–4 999	2 393	3 292	4 005	4 876	6 814	8 525
⩾5 000	583	708	977	7 142	11 079	16 500
Total for Peninsular Malaysia	12 202	15 121	17 907	14 577	21 345	29 234
Urban areas: <50	1 080	1 005	902	28	27	25
50–249	2 466	2 865	3 125	335	396	432
250–999	3 145	4 048	4 613	1 692	2 209	2 548
1 000–4 999	2 071	2 803	3 670	4 333	5 965	7 760
⩾5 000	423	683	977	6 135	10 878	16 501
Total for urban areas	9 185	11 404	13 287	12 523	19 475	27 266

Source: Malaysia *Census of Distributive Trades* Department of Statistics, various years

Table 6.4 Wholesale establishments by employment size, Peninsular Malaysia

Employment size group	No. of establishments			Value of output ($Mm.)		
	1974	1978	1980	1974	1978	1980
Peninsular Malaysia: <10 persons	10 077	12 516	14 919	5 457	7 593	10 049
10–49 persons	1 987	2 425	2 801	6 553	9 147	12 260
50–99 persons	89	115	112	1 381	1 907	2 469
⩾100 persons	49	65	75	1 186	2 697	4 458
Total for Peninsular Malaysia	12 202	15 121	7 907	14 577	21 344	29 236
Urban areas: <10 persons	7 282	9 046	10 579	3 967	6 295	8 498
10–49 persons	1 765	2 178	2 521	5 989	8 576	11 842
50–99 persons	89	115	112	1 381	1 907	2 469
⩾100 persons	49	65	75	1 186	2 697	4 458
Total for urban areas	9 185	11 404	13 287	12 523	19 475	27 267

Source: Malaysia *Census of Distributive Trades* Department of Statistics, various years

Table 6.5 Structure of wholesale establishments, Peninsular Malaysia

Type of business	No. of establishments			Value of output ($Mm.)		
	1974	1978	1980	1974	1978	1980
Perishable foodstuffs (meat, poultry, fish & vegetables)	1 259	1 375	1 591	539	736	1 053
Non-perishable foodstuffs	2 230	2 415	2 634	3 468	4 176	4 857
Tobacco & liquor	385	318	548	748	924	1 657
Domestic hardware, appliances & furnishings	549	825	966	507	1 062	1 824
Apparel (clothing, textile & footwear)	799	824	883	708	907	1 193
Personal goods* (chemists' goods, stationery & jewellery)	1 073	1 360	1 422	678	1 085	1 431
Transport vehicles (bicycles, motor vehicles & parts)	1 128	2 072	2 524	1 254	2 021	2 913
Petrol sellers	189	269	324	998	2 218	3 660
Industrial & agricultural equipment and machinery	667	1 187	1 467	751	1 505	2 161
Lumber & building materials	1 969	2 727	3 663	1 766	3 035	4 464
Agricultural products & livestock	703	510	286	404	522	580
Chemicals & fertilisers	432	361	557	952	884	997
Fuel, mineral metal & other merchants	705	811	977	315	834	819
Large general wholesalers	109	67	65	1 491	1 436	1 614
Total	12 202	15 121	17 907	14 579	21 345	29 236

Source: Malaysia *Survey of Distributive Trades* Department of Statistics, various years
*Includes household and personal goods

consumption by stores, department stores, mail order houses, retail motor vehicle dealers, consumer cooperatives and auction houses. Retailers in Malaysia also include authorised or appointed agents who sell on account of others, on consignment or commission basis, such as motor vehicle agents, self-employed retail agents and brokers selling on account of others and rental of household and personal goods and repair services.

In 1980, retail outlets in Peninsular Malaysia recorded an average annual output of $M134 000. The average output value of retail outlets in the urban areas was more than 10 times that of their counterparts in the rural areas; the output values being $M600 000 and $M54 000 respectively. Table 6.6 shows that 60 per cent of retail stores in Peninsular Malaysia had an output size of below $M50 000 in 1980, and less than 2 per cent had an output size of above $1.0 m. In the urban areas the output size of most retail establishments exceeded $M50 000 and in over 11 per cent of these establishments there was an output in excess of $M1.0 m. In addition, many retail outlets depended on family workers or had few employees; 93 per cent of the retail establishments in Peninsular Malaysia employed less than five people and less than 1 per cent employed more than 20 people (see table 6.7).

The above indicates the multiplicity of small intermediaries at the retail level and the presence of intensive and long channels of distribution. The most common form of retailing outlets are the independent traders or stores such as provision and grocery shops. They are found in virtually every town and village, and carry an assortment of stock, but in small quantities, to serve the local clientele. These shops keep long hours and depend mostly on family members to run the operations. The store-premises are extensively utilised with limited emphasis on display and decor.

The larger stores, employing more than 20 people and having an output exceeding $M1.0 m., are mostly located in the urban centres. Large-scale retailing, such as department stores and emporiums, are well accepted by the more affluent urban residents. They are becoming an increasingly important form of retailing for the future. In addition, supermarkets specialising in groceries and general household goods have also gained popularity in the larger urban centres and affluent suburbs. As many families with working wives opt for the convenience and more attractive surroundings of the supermarkets, many of these 'supermarkets' have expanded their range to include electrical and other specialised stores. Their appeal lies not in their pricing but in the wide assortment of goods available, and the comfortable surroundings and 'modern' image projected.

Shopping complexes are another fairly recent phenomenon in the retail end of the Malaysian distribution system. Again, they are located mainly in the urban centres and suburban residential areas.

Table 6.6 Retail establishments by output size, Peninsular Malaysia

Output size group ($M 0 000s)	No. of establishments			Value of output ($Mm.)		
	1974	1978	1980	1974	1978	1980
Peninsular Malaysia: <50	55 708	52 225	53 534	909	1 063	1 192
50–249	13 367	17 196	29 140	1 430	1 779	3 021
250–999	2 899	4 267	5 715	1 365	1 955	2 710
1 000–4 999	484	1 033	1 449	831	1 869	2 760
⩾5 000	47	117	199	466	1 258	2 424
Total for Peninsular Malaysia	72 505	74 838	90 037	5 001	7 924	12 107
Urban areas: <249	4 334	6 144	7 826	570	199	1 030
250–999	2 205	2 970	3 985	1 061	1 431	1 894
1 000–4 999	404	897	1 324	739	1 665	2 577
⩾5 000	47	117	199	466	1 259	2 424
Total for urban areas	6 990	10 128	13 334	2 836	4 554	7 925

Source: Malaysia *Census of Distributive Trades* Department of Statistics, various years

Table 6.7 Retail establishments by employment size, Peninsular Malaysia

Employment size group	No. of establishments			Value of output ($Mm.)		
	1974	1978	1980	1974	1978	1980
Peninsular Malaysia: <5 persons	68 052	69 950	83 962	2 471	3 574	5 366
5–19 persons	4 220	4 552	5 718	1 724	2 095	4 125
20–99 persons	213	289	306	628	789	2 008
100–499 persons	20	47	51	177	286	609
Total for Peninsular Malaysia	72 505	74 838	90 037	5 000	6 744	12 108
Urban areas: <5 persons	4 196	6 666	9 470	722	1 259	2 022
5–19 persons	2 561	3 138	3 507	1 308	2 220	3 287
20–99 persons	213	277	306	628	1 234	2 008
≥100–499 persons	20	47	51	177	442	609
Total for urban areas	6 990	10 728	13 334	2 835	5 155	7 926

Source: Malaysia *Census of Distributive Trades* Department of Statistics, various years

These complexes are in actual fact a collection of independent stores, generally small in size, housed under the comfort of a large air-conditioned complex with one or two large 'anchor stores' to pull in the crowd. The small stores in these complexes then generally try to cater to the specialised needs of the customers attracted in by the 'anchor stores'.

Finally there are the few manufacturers who have established their own branch stores in an attempt to reap the benefits of large volumes and economies-of-scale. For example, Bata has its own chain of stores all over the country to market Bata shoes.

All these point to a trend towards large-scale retailing in the urban centres. As the concept and benefits of large-scale retailing become more apparent and widely accepted, it promises to be the trend for the future. Structural changes in the retail end of the Malaysian distribution system are clearly taking place. Emporiums and 'supermarkets' are sprouting up in both major and minor urban areas. In the major urban centres, shopping complexes are appearing in practically every residential suburb to cater to the needs of the people. All this could mean a gradual decline of the smaller and traditional retail outlets in the urban centres, unless these outlets can adopt new marketing techniques in response to these changes.

In addition, joint ventures between local entrepreneurs and well-known foreign names are gaining in popularity in the establishment of retail outlets. In Kuala Lumpur, for example, Japanese well-known names such as Kimisawa have set up joint-venture supermarkets; similarly, the French retailing chain Printemps has also set-up joint-venture operations. These have resulted in greater competition to current retail outlets. Such joint ventures have succeeded in injecting a new flavour into the local retailing scene, as well as the transfer of foreign and proven expertise to the local retailing business. It is also in line with the more cosmopolitan outlook of Malaysian urban residents.

With respect to the structure of the retailing business, table 6.8 shows that the food sector had the highest output value of $M3 979 m. (33 per cent of total $M12 107 m.) in 1980. This was retailed from 61 360 outlets. The average annual output per outlet was $M65 000. The transport vehicles and parts business recorded an output value of $M2 646 m. while apparels accounted for $M1 419 m. in 1980. They were retailed from 3 192 and 7 195 outlets respectively. In the urban centres of Peninsular Malaysia, the food sector alone accounted for 15.7 per cent of the total retail output value. There were 5 186 retail outlets in the urban areas; and the average annual output value was $M240 000 per outlet, almost five times that of retail outlets in the rural areas ($M49 000). Food retailing outlets in the urban areas are generally large and employ more people while those in the rural areas are generally smaller and have a more restricted clientele. Apparel

Table 6.8 Structure of retail establishments, Peninsular Malaysia

Type of business	No. of establishments			Value of output ($Mm.)		
	1974	1978	1980	1974	1978	1980
Perishable foodstuffs (meat, poultry, fish & vegetables)	15 602	14 792	15 230	334	535	709
Non-perishable foodstuffs	33 123	37 568	46 130	1 454	2 018	3 270
Tobacco & liquor	1 235	856	797	31	90	62
Domestic hardware, appliances & furnishings	4 365	5 349	6 774	550	952	1 438
Apparel (clothing, textile & footwear)	6 784	5 431	7 195	629	1 029	1 419
Personal goods* (chemists' goods, stationery & jewellery)	6 812	7 322	9 403	487	760	1 181
Transport vehicles (bicycles, motor vehicles & parts)	3 319	2 525	3 304	948	1 744	2 646
Petrol, lubricants, oils etc.	1 265	995	1 204	568	797	1 382
Total	72 505	74 838	90 037	5 001	7 925	12 107

Source: Malaysia *Survey of Distributive Trades* Department of Statistics, various years
*Includes household and personal goods

trade in the urban areas accounted for 77.5 per cent of the total apparel retailing business in Peninsular Malaysia, indicating the greater emphasis that urban residents place on dressing and their greater spending power, compared to rural residents. The other important retailing sectors are the personal goods sector (for goods such as stationery and jewellery), and domestic hardware appliances and furnishings.

Establishment and location of retailing outlets

The establishment and location of retailing outlets crucially depend on the types of products and modes of outlets that are desired. *Departmental stores* are designed to sell a wide variety of merchandise, including piece-goods, home furnishings, and furniture. They are based on the concept of large sales volume, generated by attractive decor and display and moderate to high margins. These stores are large and are typically located in downtown shopping districts or in newer shopping centres. They are present in all the major urban centres in Malaysia, for example, Metro and Printemps in Kuala Lumpur, Gamma in Penang and Super Kinta in Ipoh.

Specialty stores retail a broad selection of a restricted class of goods. They are usually small to medium-sized establishments, handling limited lines of goods. Specialty stores, retailing imported products or high fashion/well-known brand goods, are gaining increasing popularity among the affluent middle-class residents. Such stores are generally located in exclusive shopping centres in the major urban centres.

The *chain store* system first started during pre-Independence days and thcy dcalt mainly with houschold and pcrsonal items. The best-known chain store in Malaysia is Emporium Holdings, with a chain of 11 stores spread all over Peninsular Malaysia. Their goods are competitively priced due to savings in their bulk-buying power and higher managerial efficiency.

Supermarkets, such as Jaya Supermarkets, in Malaysia offer an attractive alternative to the traditional wet-markets and sundry shops. They offer comfortable air-conditioned convenient shopping and the goods are well displayed. The goods retailed include a relatively broad and complete stock of dry groceries, fresh meat, perishable products, and dairy products, supplemented by a variety of convenient, non-food merchandise. The supermarkets appeal to the higher income clientele as their pricing is generally higher, although discounts and other promotions are regularly used.

Shopping complexes are integrated developments under single ownership, with coordinated and complete shopping facilities, and adequate parking space. The stores in the centre are leased to various retailers who may deal in specialty or general goods. There is an abundance of shopping centres in the major urban centres in Peninsular Malaysia, such as Sungai Wang Plaza and Yow Chuan Plaza in Kuala Lumpur, Pulau Pinang Plaza and KOMTAR in Penang, and Kompleks Tun Abdul Razak in Johore Bahru. These shopping complexes have generally been very successful; in fact the rental value in centres such as Sungai Wang Plaza is among the highest of all property rentals.

Non-store retailing has also made its appearance in Malaysia although on a small scale. Automatic merchandisers utilising vending machines offering soft drinks in packets or in bottles, are the most common. However, the machines are expensive to maintain, requiring considerable stocking time as well as labour. The goods are, therefore, priced slightly higher than their corresponding prices elsewhere as larger margins are necessary. The assortment of products marketed are limited, as only stable products can be used. Yeo Hiap Seng (a local soft-drink manufacturer) currently uses vending machines to dispense its soft drinks at petrol stations, entertainment centres and shopping centres.

The retailing of goods through *mail order* has to date not been very successful and is limited to books by Readers' Digest, and various items by credit card companies such as the American Express.

Direct selling is gaining popularity in Malaysia. The pioneers in this field were Tupperware using the 'home-party' system, and Amway selling its products through the distributors' system. The crux of this retail method is the recruitment of a large number of distributors so as to generate more sales. While overhead costs are relatively low for such operations, generous mark-ups have to be given to the distributors to encourage sales. The location of the company's premises is based mainly on convenience to the distributors. Though the set-up cost of a direct selling establishment is relatively low, this system has yet to acquire massive success; the general population has not acquired the level of confidence towards these retailers to enable them to 'direct-sell' easily.

The largest retail outlets in Peninsular Malaysia are located in Kuala Lumpur, Petaling Jaya, Ipoh, Penang, Johore Bahru and Kuantan. Residents in such areas are receptive to the latest innovations and concepts in retailing. This is mainly due to the fact that there is a larger proportion of affluent people in these urban centres, who seek convenience and whose opportunity cost for time is high.

The initial investment for establishing large retail stores is high, as large and well-decorated stores are needed to attract the clientele. The Long John Silver (a seafood chain) outlet in the Sungai Wang Plaza in Kuala Lumpur required about $M1.0 m. in equipment and decor. There is also a need for advertising to generate community goodwill and awareness among the population, while regular promotions are needed to increase the store traffic. For the well-managed stores linked to well-known brand names, past experiences have shown that they can be extremely profitable ventures. The Malaysia population, particularly the urbanites, are extremely cosmopolitan; they are generally very receptive to new innovations in marketing which give them value for their money and time.

7

Procedures and incentives for business

An investor, whether foreign or local, wishing to participate in a business activity in Malaysia has generally to incorporate a company in Malaysia. Further, an intended investor wishing to set up an industrial enterprise in Malaysia is also required to apply for a manufacturing licence from the Ministry of Trade and Industry. On receipt of the licence the investor should incorporate a local company with the Registrar of Companies and then apply for the necessary land from the appropriate state authorities to build the needed manufacturing facility. In this chapter, I will discuss the legislations governing the procedure for the establishment of a manufacturing facility and the procedures governing the operation of other enterprises.

Manufacturing licence

The 1975 Industrial Coordination Act stipulates that no person shall engage in any manufacturing activity with a pay-up capital in excess of $M250 000 capital or an employment of over 25 persons, unless he or she is issued a licence by the Ministry of Trade and Industry for such an activity. In the issuance of such licence, general conditions regarding the structure of the corporate equity and employment are imposed; these conditions are to ensure that the new company would make every attempt to conform to the spirit of the NEP which requires that a substantial proportion of the equity be held by the Bumiputras (30 per cent) and other Malaysians (40 per cent) and that the workforce should reflect the racial composition of the country.

When the Act was first introduced considerable controversy was generated, particularly by the requirement that all existing manufacturing establishments had to apply for the licence. The business community then viewed it as an instrument through which the government could impose its desire to restructure the industrial sector.

However, subsequent amendments to the Act which allow for appeals by investors regarding the conditions imposed on the licence, as well as subsequent experience by the business community concerning the speed and flexibility with which the licences were issued, tended to alleviate this concern.

Registration of companies

On receipt of the manufacturing licence, the interested industrial investor should incorporate a local company with the Registrar of Companies. It should be pointed out that for the non-industrial investor such a licence is, of course, not needed for the incorporation of the local company. The 1975 Company Act provides the procedure for the incorporation of a company with limited liabilities, and the running of the company after its incorporation. Further details on the incorporation of company can be found in the relevant Act; in general, this Act follows the standard British practice of company incorporation and management.

Registration of trade marks and patents

Trade marks and patents are registered in Malaysia, and governed by the provision of the Trade Mark Ordinance which is implemented in Peninsular Malaysia and Sabah and Sarawak. Registration of patents is governed by the United Kingdom Patent Ordinance. Application for the registration of a trade mark can be made on the prescribed forms which are provided free by the Ministry of Trade and Industry. Foreign applicants are required to submit their application through a local agent. Trade mark registration is effective for seven years with possible renewal of a further 28 years.

Application for industrial land

In Malaysia, land is under the review of the state governments. This implies that all applications for land to construct manufacturing facilities should be made through one of two processes:

1 purchase of a suitable existing manufacturing facility from another industrialist who is willing to sell the manufacturing facility;

2 to apply to the State Economics Development Corporation (SEDC) of a particular state for a vacant industrial lot (these are generally located in industrial estates developed by the SEDCs); the location, availability, and price of this land is

given in the schedule of industrial estates available from the Malaysian Industrial Development Authority.

Experience shows that all applications for industrial land can be processed fairly speedily by the SEDCs. In most cases decisions are made within six months to a year.

Employment of personnel

Employment is governed by the 1955 Employment Ordinance Act which sets out minimum terms and conditions of employment in the country. It is applicable to all manual and non-manual workers with earnings less than $M750 per month. This Ordinance specifies the time-frame for payment of wages, period for notices of termination, working hours and overtime rates and leave entitlements. However, one important feature of the Ordinance is that there is no minimum wage for employees in Malaysia. Notwithstanding this, because of rapid economic development, wages are generally fairly uniform across industrial sectors; in general a skilled worker is paid about $M500 per month, a unskilled worker about $M250 per month, and managerial personnel, about $M1 000–$M2 000 per month.

The employment of children and young persons is governed by the Child and Young Persons Employment Act 1966. This Act rigidly controls the conditions under which children (persons less than 14 years of age) and young persons (persons 14–16 years of age) can be employed. The main intention of the Act is to guarantee the safety of these persons in employment, as well as to ensure that they are not exploited in the work situation.

The Employee Provident Act provides a fund scheme for the payment of cash benefits to an employee when he/she has attained the age of 55 years or in the event of his/her total incapacity or permanent departure from the country. All employers are required to register their employees with the Fund and to ensure that monthly contributions are made according to the table of prescribed rates. Currently, the employee's share of the contribution is 9 per cent of his/her monthly wage while the employer's share is 11 per cent.

Taxation

Income of an individual is taxable if it accrues in or is derived from Malaysia whether or not the individual is resident in Malaysia. A resident individual (for tax purposes) is liable to tax on income from outside sources that is received in Malaysia.

Resident status is determined by reference to the duration of stay in Malaysia. Generally a person is a tax resident if he/she is in Malaysia for more than 182 days.

Income from employment exercised for a period or periods which together do not exceed 60 days in a calendar year is exempt from tax. This does not apply to professional entertainers and non-resident directors of companies resident in Malaysia.

Employment exercised for less than 183 days is taxed at 40 per cent on the full amount of emoluments (except where specifically provided otherwise under any tax treaty). The liability of an area representative is generally computed on the basis of time spent in Malaysia or the income remitted into the country whichever is the greater. The schedule of personal income tax is given in table 7.1.

Company tax

A company resident in Malaysia is assessable to tax on income accruing in or derived from or received in Malaysia. A non-resident company is assessable on income accruing in, or derived from Malaysia, but not on income received in Malaysia from outside sources.

A company is considered resident where its control and management are exercised in Malaysia and control is generally considered to be the place where the directors' meetings are held.

Table 7.1 Schedule of personal income tax

Chargeable income ($)	*Tax rates* (%)		($)	*Proposed tax payable* ($)
1– 2 500	5	on the first	2 500	125
2 501– 5 000	8	on the next	2 500	200
		on the first	5 000	325
5 001– 10 000	12	on the next	5 000	600
		on the first	10 000	925
10 001– 20 000	15	on the next	10 000	1 500
		on the first	20 000	2 425
20 001– 35 000	20	on the next	15 000	3 000
		on the first	35 000	5 425
35 001– 50 000	25	on the next	15 000	3 750
		on the first	50 000	9 175
50 001– 70 000	30	on the next	20 000	6 000
		on the first	70 000	15 175
70 001–100 000	35	on the next	30 000	10 500
		on the first	100 000	25 675
Above 100 000	40			

Exceeding $300 000—excess profit tax at 5 per cent
Source: New Straits Times 20 October 1984

The rate of tax on taxable income for resident and non-resident companies is 40 per cent. A development tax of five per cent is also payable. Where taxable income exceeds a prescribed limit (minimum of $M200 000), excess profits tax at five per cent is also payable on such excess.

Taxable income is assessable income less allowable deductions. These deductions include:

1 expenditure wholly and exclusively incurred in the production of the income being assessed
2 capital allowances for assets owned and used for the purpose of producing income
3 losses and unabsorbed capital allowances from prior periods. There are no provisions for carry back
4 interest on money borrowed and employed in producing income provided that, when the interest is paid to a non-resident, withholding tax of 15 per cent has been deducted (unless relieved under a tax treaty or specifically exempted)
5 royalties if wholly and exclusively incurred in producing the income being assessed and provided that, where the royalty is paid to a non-resident, withholding tax of 15 per cent has been deducted (unless relieved under a tax treaty or specifically exempted)
6 where intercompany services are provided, the charge will be deductible if the companies are operating at arm's length and the charges are fair. Payments to non-residents may be subject to a withholding tax of 15 per cent depending on the type of services.

The cumulative income tax less tax reliefs that has been paid on company profits may be imputed to dividends paid to shareholders. The tax available for this purpose is the accumulated balance of tax paid, less any amount already imputed to dividends.

Provisions against future losses or expenditure which have not been actually incurred are not allowable deductions.

The basis for a year of assessment is the calendar year immediately preceding the year of assessment. The basis period is normally the same as a basis year. But if the annual accounts of a business are made up to some date other than 31 December, the basis period for the business source will be the 12 months ended in the basis year.

Incentives for industrial investment

The country offers attractive incentives to both foreign and local investors who make investments consistent with its industrialisation programme.

Malaysia's industrial investment incentives, under the 1968 Investment Incentives Act, were designed to provide relief from the payment of various forms of taxes. Companies in the country are normally subjected to 40 per cent company tax, 5 per cent development tax and an excess profit tax of 5 per cent. Companies enjoying tax relief incentives are exempted from the above taxes. Further, dividends declared by such companies are also tax-exempted. However, there are cases where companies enjoy partial tax relief which may be in the form of export allowance and accelerated or depreciation allowances. In such instances, the companies involved are only partially tax-exempted and not fully exempted from tax.

The major forms of tax incentives under the 1968 Investment Incentive Act, are as follows:

Pioneer status

Pioneer status may be granted to any kind of commercial or industrial undertaking. It is intended particularly for companies which intend to produce goods not already manufactured on a commercial scale in the country or whose establishment is vital to the public interest (see appendix 2 for list of priority products). Companies which intend to manufacture their products wholly for export are also generally considered as a pioneer enterprise.

Companies given pioneer status are allowed an initial tax-relief period of two to five years, beginning on production day. Table 7.2 shows the tax-free holiday period for different categories of companies.

In addition to the above, an extension of a further year of tax relief is granted for each of the following three conditions fulfilled. This

Table 7.2 Pioneer status: tax-free period for different categories of companies

Tax-free period (Years)	Companies eligible
2	Companies with capital investments less than $M250 000
3	Companies with capital investments not less than $M250 000
4	Companies with capital investments not less than $M500 000
5	Companies with capital investments not less than $M1 m.

brings the maximum tax-holiday period to eight years. The three conditions are as follows:

1 if the pioneer factory is sited in a development area. The government has declared the states of Kedah, Perlis, Pahang, Kelantan, Trengganu, Malacca, Sabah and Sarawak and the industrial estates Senawang, Kamunting, Sungai Way, Bayan Lepas, Ulu Klang, Tanjung Agas and Senai as development areas. Further, the Ministry of Trade and Industry has the power to declare any specific areas in the States of Selangor, Johor, Penang, Perak and Negeri Sembilan as development areas
2 if the product/industry is a priority product or industry. A list of such priority products has been approved by the Minister of Trade and Industry and the Minister of Finance. A copy of the list can be found in appendix 2
3 if the specified Malaysian content is attained. A product can qualify for this additional incentive if it incorporates at least 50 per cent, by value, of Malaysian raw materials and or parts and components manufactured in Malaysia excluding wages, salaries and other non-traded service inputs.

Labour utilisation relief

The labour utilisation relief provides for exemption from income tax and development tax by the company. The granting of such exemption is similar to that under pioneer status except that the basis of exemption is based upon the number of full-time paid employees engaged in the project. This incentive is also designed to encourage industrial ventures to generate greater employment opportunities in the country.

Table 7.3 shows the tax-exemptions period and their qualifying requirements.

Besides this, an extension of a further year of tax-relief period is granted for each of the conditions listed under sub-sections (i), (ii) and (iii) above fulfilled.

Table 7.3 Labour utilisation relief: tax exemption period and the qualifying requirements

Tax-free period (Years)	Qualifying employment
2	51–100 employees
3	101–200 employees
4	201–350 employees
5	351 and more employees

Locational incentive

This incentive was introduced to encourage the decentralisation of industrial activities in the urban areas. Any approved company locating its factory in an area specified by the government as a Locational Incentive Area may be granted a maximum tax relief of up to 10 years. The following areas have been declared as Locational Incentive Areas:

the state of Kedah, excluding the Kuala Muda District
the state of Pahang, excluding the Kuantan District
the whole state of Kelantan
the whole state of Trengganu
the whole state of Perlis
the whole state of Sabah
the whole state of Sarawak
the Johor Tenggara Area.

The qualifying criteria and number of years of tax are as shown in table 7.4.

Where losses are incurred by the company for the whole of its tax-relief period, the total amount would be allowed to be deducted from assessable income earned in the post tax-free period.

Table 7.4 Locational incentive: qualifying criteria and number of years of tax relief

Qualifying level of fixed capital expenditure/full-time employment	Tax exemption period (Years)
For companies with fixed capital expenditure less than $M250 000 or employment less than 101	5
For companies with fixed capital expenditure not less than $M250 000 or employment not less than 101	6
For companies with fixed capital expenditure not less than $M500 000 or employment not less than 201	7
For companies with fixed capital expenditure not less than $M1 m. or employment not less than 351	8
Priority product	1
Malaysian product	1
Total number of years of tax relief	10

Investment tax credit

The investment tax credit can be granted to companies not enjoying pioneer status. Companies benefiting from the Utilisation Relief or the Locational Incentives are also excluded from this provision. The benefit given to a company that is granted the investment tax credit is in the form of exemptions of income tax on profits which is equal to the tax credit given. The amount of tax credit given will not be less than 25 per cent of the total capital expenditure incurred in the project. It is given for the year of assessment in the basis period in which the expenditure was incurred and for not more than five years after the beginning of the basis period in which the project was approved.

An additional five per cent deduction is granted for each of the following conditions fulfilled:

if the factory is in a development area
if it produces a priority product
if the specified percentage of Malaysian content is attained.

Export incentives

The three kinds of export incentives granted by the Malaysian government to manufacturing companies are:

Export allowance The formula used for computing the allowance is

i For a company which is already exporting
x*2% plus (x-y)* 10%

ii For a company which is exporting for the first time
x*12%

where,

x = ex-factory value of exports in the basis period
y = ex-factory value of exports of the year in which the company was last exporting.

Accelerated depreciation allowance Only resident companies which export 20 per cent of the value of their total production and incur qualifying plant expenditures for the purpose of modernising company production techniques, or setting up a modernised factory, are entitled to this allowance. Companies granted this allowance are permitted an accelerated depreciation allowance of 40 per cent per annum in addition to the initial allowance of 20 per cent.

Deductions for promotion overseas Deductions are given for expenses incurred for the purpose of seeking export opportunities for made-in-Malaysia products. Expenses incurred during the tax-relief period can be carried forward and allowed as a deduction in the post tax-relief period. Expenses that qualify for this deduction are:

overseas advertising;
supply of free samples abroad;

marketing research on exports;
preparation of tenders for the supply of goods overseas;
supply of technical information abroad;
public relations work connected with export;
expenses directly contributable to the exhibits and/or participation required in trade or industrial exhibition approved by the Minister of Trade and Industry;
fares in respect of travel overseas by employees of companies for business;
accommodation and sustenance expense incurred by Malaysian businessmen going overseas for business. This is, however, subjected to a maximum of 100 ringgit per day;
cost of maintaining sales offices overseas for the promotion of exports.

In addition to the above, export credit refinancing facility is also available for the export of goods manufactured locally; this provides Malaysian exporters with credit facilities at preferential rates of interest.

Increased capital allowance

In order to encourage existing factories to modernise their production techniques and to encourage the setting up of modern factories, the government has designed a tax incentive called the 'increased capital allowance'. The allowance can be granted to projects which the government deems to be desirable in the national interest but which cannot be granted tax exemption either under pioneer status, labour utilisation relief, locational incentives, or investment tax credit provisions.

The increased capital allowance is calculated as follows:

- for qualifying plant expenditure, the rate of capital allowance is 40 per cent;
- for qualifying building expenditure incurred on the construction is 3 per cent of that expended;
- for qualifying building expenditure incurred on the purchase of a building the permitted fraction is multiplied by 1.5.

The different incentives granted under the Investment Incentives Act 1968 are summarised in table 7.5. Further, in appendix 3 there is a summary of the procedure that should be taken by an investor for the purpose of undertaking industrial investment in Malaysia.

Table 7.5 Investment incentives act 1968

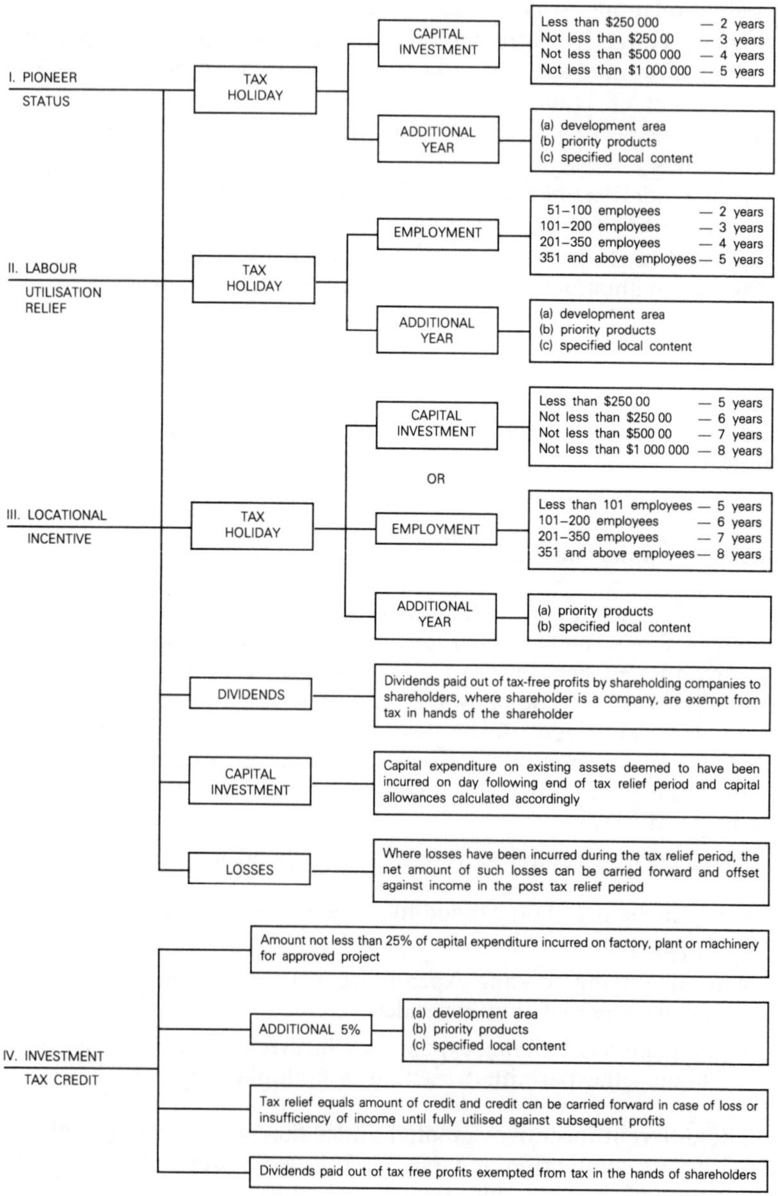

V. EXPORT INCENTIVES

- **DEDUCTIONS FOR PROMOTION OVERSEAS**

  Expenses qualified

  (a) Overseas advertising
  (b) Supply of free samples overseas
  (c) Export market research
  (d) Preparation of overseas tenders
  (e) Supply of technical information overseas
  (f) Public relations work connected with exports
  (g) Expenses directly contributable to the exhibits and/or participation required in trade or industrial exhibitions approved by the Minister of Trade and Industry
  (h) Fares in respect of travel overseas by employees of companies for business
  (i) Accommodation and sustenances expense incurred by Malaysian businessmen going overseas for business subject to $100/- per day
  (j) Cost of maintaining sales offices overseas for the promotion of exports

- **ACCELERATED DEPRECIATION ALLOWANCE**

  Only resident companies qualified
  Must export 20% by value
  Given only in respect of capital expenditure incurred on modernisation
  Rate — 40% per annum

- **EXPORT ALLOWANCE**

  Formula used:

  (i) For a company which is already exporting:
  (a) $x \times 2\%$
  plus (b) $(x - y) \times 10\%$

  (ii) For a company which is exporting for the first time:
  $x . \times 12\%$

  x = exports in the basis period
  y = exports of the year in which the company was last exporting

VI. SPECIAL INCENTIVES FOR APPROVED AGRICULTURAL INDUSTRIES

- **INVESTMENT TAX CREDIT AMOUNTING TO 50% OF QUALIFYING CAPITAL EXPENDITURE**

  Activities eligible for this incentive:

  (a) cultivation of food crops and fruits
  (b) cultivation of vegetables
  (c) rearing of fresh water fish and prawns and marine culture
  (d) rearing of livestock for meat and dairy products

VII. HOTEL INCENTIVES

Pioneer status; accelerated depreciation allowance; industrial building allowance (with the exception of K.L. District and Penang Island); abatement of income tax on a percentage of chargeable income (depending on hotel location) for a period of 12 years

VIII. INCREASED CAPITAL ALLOWANCE

- **CAPITAL ALLOWANCE**

  (a) for qualifying plant expenditure, the rate of capital allowance is 40%
  (b) for qualifying building expenditure incurred on the construction of a building, the capital allowance is 3% of that expenditure
  (c) for qualifying building expenditure incurred on the purchase of a building, the permitted fraction is multiplied by $1\frac{1}{2}$

Source: Malaysia *Investment Incentives Act 1968 (Revised—1978)* Kuala Lumpur: Malaysian Industrial Development Authority, 1980, 1–2
Note: The incentives incorporate all the amendments up to 1 September 1980

Other tax incentives for business

Hotel incentives are granted to businessmen who wish to set up hotels/motels and tourist resort complexes. It is also offered for the expansion and modernisation of existing hotels. The type of incentives offered and the extent of such incentives depend, however, on the location of approved hotels. Approved hotels located in the areas specified below will be granted the following incentives:

	Area		*Incentives*
A	KL District and Penang Island	(i)	pioneer status; or abatement of income tax on 15 per cent of chargeable income for a period of 12 years and accelerated depreciation allowance The above only applies to hotels that are completed and open for business between the periods 1 January 1968 and 31 December 1973
B	Selangor (other than KL District) Perak, Negeri Sembilan, Malacca, Johore and Kota Kinabalu	(i)	pioneer status; or abatement of income tax on 20 per cent of chargeable income for a period of 12 years and accelerated depreciation allowance
		(ii)	industrial building allowance
C	Pahang, Trengganu, Kedah, Kelantan, Perlis, East Malaysia except Kota Kinabalu	(i)	pioneer status; or abatement of income tax on 25 per cent of chargeable income for a period of 12 years
D	Island, hill resorts and other designated areas	(i)	pioneer status; or abatement of income tax on 30 per cent of chargeable income for a period of 12 years and accelerated depreciation allowance; or hotel tax credit
		(ii)	industrial building allowance

The granting and continued operation of the above incentives will be conditional upon government being satisfied, *inter alia*, of the following:

the standard of management and service in approved hotels and the maintenance of the standards specified for luxury, first and medium-class hotels; and the rates for rooms and other services charged in these hotels.

The tax-relief period for companies which are granted pioneer status will be effective from the date of commencement of the new business or in the case of expansion or modernisation of an existing hotel from the date of completion of such expansion or modernisation.

For hotels which are granted abatement of chargeable income, the abatement will apply from the year of assessment following the date of commencement of the new business or, in the case of expansion or modernisation of an existing hotel, from the year of assessment following the date of completion of such expansion or modernisation.

Special incentives for approved agricultural industries Investment tax credit amounting to 50 per cent of the qualifying capital expenditure on approved agricultural industries can be granted to stimulate greater and better utilisation of agricultural land. Initially the activities eligible include cultivation of food crops, marine culture and dairy farming.

The following incentives can also be granted to companies engaged in cultivation of approved crops.

1 allowance at 50 per cent of the expenditure incurred in clearing, planting, preparing of estates and construction of roads is given for two years of assessment
2 expenditure incurred in building of labourers' quarters is eligible for an allowance of 20 per cent given for five years
3 expenditure incurred on the construction of buildings used in the working of the estates is written off over 10 years at 10 per cent per annum
4 expenditure incurred on replanting will be allowed as a revenue expenditure
5 plant and machinery used in the extraction of timber from a forest is eligible for an increased initial allowance of 60 per cent instead of the present 20 per cent.

Reinvestment allowance All existing manufacturing companies not enjoying any incentives granted under the Investment Incentives Act (except for export incentives) or who have ceased to enjoy them for at least three years, are eligible to apply for reinvestment allowance. It is given at 25 per cent of the expenditure on factory, plant and machinery, and industrial building incurred for expansion during the basis period for assessment years 1980 to 1986. The reinvestment allowance is administered directly by the Income Tax Department, but before companies can avail themselves of this incentive, their expansion programmes must first have been approved by the Ministry of Trade and Industry unless they are exempted under the Industrial Coordination Act.

The accelerated depreciation allowance in the form of an annual allowance of 80 per cent of plant and machinery (which is different from the normal annual allowance), is accorded to all industries for expenditures incurred during the basis period of assessment years 1978 to 1986 to encourage the establishment, modernisation and expansion of industrial activities. Hence, economic activities undertaken between 1977 and 1985 would qualify for this concession. The annual allowance of 80 per cent is granted in lieu of the previous allowances prescribed in the Income Tax (Qualifying Plant Annual Allowance) Rules, 1968. With the initial allowance of 20 per cent unchanged, 100 per cent or the entire amount of the capital cost plant and machinery is, thus, allowed to be written off in one year for tax purposes.

Restructuring incentives There are two types of tax incentives for restructuring introduced under the 1980 budget to accelerate the pace of restructuring and the promotion of investment and economic growth.

1 equity restructuring when companies conform to the equity restructuring requirement of NEP with at least 30 per cent equity for Bumiputra, 40 per cent for non-Bumiputra Malaysians and 30 per cent for foreigners, these are granted exemptions of five percentage points of the company income tax of 40 per cent.
2 employment and/or marketing network restructuring exemption of the five per cent development tax is granted to companies in Malaysia that have:
    a an employment structure which reflects the racial composition of the country's population in all grades of appointment up to managerial level, and/or
    b at least 30 per cent of its sales in the domestic market allocated to Bumiputra distributors

The incentives for restructuring are offered on a yearly basis for three years of assessment starting from 1980. To qualify the company must have either paid-up capital (unimpaired by contingent liability) or a net asset (before revaluation) of not less than $M1m. Pioneer companies and companies enjoying tax incentives are not eligible for these incentives.

Exemption from withholding tax The Income Tax Act provides for the deduction of withholding tax at 15 per cent on interest and royalty payable to a non-resident who does not have a place of business in Malaysia. The amount payable by way of interest or royalty is exempt from withholding tax if it is paid in respect of an approved loan or royalty or a long-term loan.

A long-term loan is one with a term of not less than three years where the funds are remitted from outside Malaysia by a non-resident. An approved loan is one which is for specified purposes and approved by the government. Licensed banks in Malaysia are not required to deduct withholding tax on interest paid or credited to non-residents except where the interest paid or credited is on funds required for the purposes of maintaining net working funds.

Incentives for the shipping industry A scheme of tax incentives has been introduced to encourage the growth of the shipping industry in Malaysia. Income tax relief is given for a period of 24 years for Malaysian resident shipping companies commencing from the year of assessment 1982 or the date of incorporation, whichever is the later. For the first 12 years, such companies will be fully exempt from income tax. In the next 12 years, the companies will be eligible for a 50 per cent abatement of chargeable income in each year of assessment. The profits thus exempted or abated can be utilised for declaring dividends which will be tax exempt in the shareholders' hands. However, a company must satisfy the following conditions during the period of enjoyment of the incentive:

1 the total of tax exempt dividends declared in a year of assessment should not exceed 15 per cent of the paid-up capital on the first day of the basis period
2 a company must use at least 75 per cent of the fleet acquisition reserve during specified parts of the period for the purchase of ships or vessels

The fleet acquisition reserve is the excess of the audited net profit of the company over the dividends and/or tax payable.

Additional incentives for exports

1 A manufacturer is entitled to claim drawback of import duty on the export of finished goods and surtax on any raw materials and components used in the manufacture of the export products. The manufacturer must import the components in order to be eligible for drawback.
2 Nine-tenths of the import duty and surtax paid is recoverable on the re-export of the imported goods. These goods should not be put into use after importation.
3 Incentives under Excise Act Again to relieve the burden of local taxes on export goods, excisable goods for export fulfilling certain conditions are exempted from excise duty. In addition, drawback of excise duty is allowed on raw materials used in the manufacture of specified export goods. At present, drawback is allowed only for imports of sugar and intoxicating liquor used in the specified products.
4 Incentives under Sales Tax Act a no sales tax is payable on the export of goods; b drawback of sales tax is granted on export of indigenous goods on which sales tax was paid and on re-export of imported goods

5 Export refinancing facility This facility, implemented in 1977, is designed to encourage the export of goods (except petroleum products) manufactured in Malaysia and to provide Malaysian exporters with credit facilities at preferential rates of interest. Under this scheme, all export insurance bills of exchange (bills with a period to run before being due for payment) are eligible for financing by commercial banks at 7 per cent rate of interest. In providing this facility, the central bank, Bank Negara, has undertaken to subsidise the commercial banks by refinancing them at a rate of 5.5 per cent per annum. This credit is granted for a maximum of 90 days and the Malaysian dollar equivalent of an export bill should not be less than $M20 000.

The availability of finance at a concessional rate of interest helps reduce the cost of financing exports. This, in turn, contributes to an overall reduction in costs, making Malaysian export products more competitive. It also enables a Malaysian exporter to extend longer credit terms to foreign importers thereby making its sales terms more attractive.

6 *Exemption from custom duties* Export-oriented companies depending exclusively on imported raw materials and components for production can obtain exemption from import duty and surtax on these components. Among other considerations, these materials must not be available locally.

7 *Manufacture for export in free trade zone* As a further measure to encourage exports, the government gives facilities to specified export-oriented industries to set up manufacturing facilities in free trade zones. The purpose is to minimise customs formalities for import of raw materials and components and export of finished goods. To date there are 10 such zones in the country (see appendix 4).

8 *Manufacture of export goods under customs bond* As an alternative to drawback of custom duties on imported raw materials and components used in the manufacture of finished export goods, the manufacturer is exempted from duties provided he/she is authorised to establish a licensed manufacturing warehouse under customs bond. To be eligible, at least 80 per cent of the total production is to be exported. Sales of any portion of its production in the domestic market should have prior approval. Import duties will be levied on such goods.

9 *Tariff protection* is given to deserving industries which are capable of supplying a major portion of the domestic market at acceptable quality and prices. In granting this, considerations are given to labour intensity, degree of utilisation of domestic raw materials and the level of local value of the final product.

10 *Import restriction* is granted where it is feared that large scale speculative imports may take place before production or as an interim measure to protect local industries or during overseas dumping.

11 *Investment Guarantee Agreements* Article 13 of the Malaysian Constitution provides guarantee against nationalisation without compensation. To give further assurance and to encourage the inflow of foreign capital, Malaysia has concluded Investment Guarantee Agreements with the United States of America, West Germany, Canada, The Netherlands, France, Switzerland, Belgo-Luxembourg, United Kingdom and Sri Lanka. Furthermore, agreements with four other countries are being negotiated.

An investment guarantee agreement normally covers:

a a guarantee that there shall be no expropriation or nationalisation except for public purposes and with prompt and adequate compensation

b permission to remit or repatriate profits, capital or other fees

c settlement of legal disputes at the International Centre for the Settlement of Investment Disputes of which Malaysia is a member.

8

New investment opportunities

As a rapidly industrialising country extensive investment opportunities exist in Malaysia for both the domestic and foreign investors. In this chapter I discuss in detail many of these investment and business opportunities.

Agricultural and fishery sectors

However Malaysia is still predominantly an agricultural and commodity producing country. In 1983 the agriculture sector contributed about 22.4 per cent of the GDP. The country is the world's largest producer of rubber and crude palm oil, one of the world's largest exporters of tropical sawn logs; producing 40 per cent of the world's output of natural rubber and 57 per cent of the world's output of crude palm oil.[1] The total hectares and production values of the major agricultural crops are given in table 8.1. With a total population of only about 15 m. people and a land area of 329 700 sq. km., extensive land resources still exist in the country for new agricultural opportunities, particularly continued investments in rubber, palm oil and new investments in pepper and cocoa plantations.

Oil palm cultivation

The oil palm sector has become an important agricultural sector since the early 1970s. The rapid development of the Malaysian oil palm industry sector began in the early 1960s when large-scale cultivation of oil palm was undertaken in agreement with the government's agricultural diversification policy away from its sole dependence on rubber. Favourable climatic condition, availability of abundant suitable land and the proper implementation of plantation strategy have enabled Malaysia to become the world's largest palm oil producer and exporter, accounting for about 80 per cent of world export of the

Table 8.1 Hectares and production of major agricultural crops

Year	Rubber Production[a]	Rubber Area[b]	Palm oil Production[a]	Palm oil Area[b]	Cocoa Production[a]	Cocoa Area[b]	Pepper Production[a]	Pepper Area[b]
1965	903	2.0	148	0.1	—	—	59	—
1970	1 269	2.0	424	0.3	—	—	—	—
1975	1 488	2.0	1 044	0.6	18	0.03	33	0.009
1980	1 552	2.0	2 573	1.0	33	0.07	32	0.010
1982	1 517	2.0	3 512	1.2	65	0.10	25	0.010

Sources: [1]Malaysia *Economic Report* Kuala Lumpur: Ministry of Finance, various years
[2]Malaysia *Annual Statistics Bulletin* Kuala Lumpur: Department of Statistics, various years
[a]Production figures in thousand tonnes
[b]Area under cultivation in million hectares

commodity in 1983. The development of the palm oil industry, which includes processing and refining, gives further impetus to the industrialisation drive of the country particularly in respect to the development of resource-based industries.

Palm oil competes with a dozen other oils and fats, including soyabean oil, rapeseed oil, coconut oil, sunflower seed oil and groundnut oil. Since there exist so many substitutes for palm oil, the key factor determining the long-term prospects for the palm oil industry is the overall world demand for oils and fats.

In fact the gradual recovery of the world economy since the early 1980s has improved the world demand for oils and fats. The demand for oils and fats are projected to grow at about 3.3 per cent per annum over the period 1980–85. The world exports of oils and fats are expected to increase at the rate of 3.7 per cent per annum,[2] with USA, EEC, Japan, India, Middle East countris, USSR and China as the major consuming markets. Within the oils and fats category, the demand for soft oil (oil produced by non-tree crops) is expected to be stronger than those for hard oils. Nevertheless, the demand for palm oil (which is an hard oil) is expected to grow at the rate of about 3.0 per cent per annum. These generally favourable market conditions for oils and fats have led to a marked improvement in the price of crude palm oil and other palm oil products since the early 1980s. For example, the average 1983 price of crude palm oil was $M991 per tonne; this represented an increase of 20 per cent over the corresponding 1982 price. The price situation for crude palm oil is expected to remain steady, if not improve, over the medium term.

Palm oil cultivation involves a gestation period of between three to four years before the palms mature enough to be productive. It is a long-term project since the economic life of the palms extends to about 25 years. Based on the assumption of an investment involving a plantation of 2 000 hectares of oil palm from virgin jungle land, with an economic life of 22 years, normal plantation costs and an average crude palm oil price of $M1 000 per tonne, the pay-back period for such an investment is seven years, with a net present value of $M6.4 m. at 14 per cent discount rate. The internal rate of return of such a project is 18 per cent.[3]

Planting palm oil is a highly profitable venture but the major problem facing an investor in this area is the acquisition of suitable land. The interested investor could overcome this problem by initiating a joint venture with an appropriate public agency which could satisfy all the requirements of NEP. Palm oil plantation is particularly attractive in land-abundant states such as Sabah, Sarawak, Pahang and Perak.

Cocoa plantation

The bulk of the world's cocoa today is produced in West Africa. In the early 1980s Malaysia became a significant producer of cocoa as a result of intensive cocoa cultivation in Sabah and some parts of Peninsular Malaysia: Malaysia's total area under cocoa plantation increased from 56 000 hectares in 1976 to 163 000 hectares in 1981. Over the period 1974–83, Malaysia's cocoa production rose from a mere 0.87 per cent to 3.53 per cent of total world production.

The demand for cocoa over the remaining part of the 1980s is projected to equal the estimated production. The developed countries would remain, by far, the largest (90 per cent) consuming market over the remaining part of the 1980s.

A major problem facing the cocoa industry is the volatility of the cocoa price. However, since 1981, cocoa price has been steadily increasing from about $M2.00 per pound (454g) to about $M2.70 per pound in 1984. Based on a cocoa estate of about 1 000 hectares, normal capital and development costs, an average cocoa price of about $M2.00 per pound of dry beans, the pay-back period for the project is about six years, with a net present value of $M2.8 million at 15 per cent discount rate and an internal rate of return of 20.5 per cent.[4] The above indicates that cocoa cultivation in Malaysia could be viable, if the price of cocoa does not fluctuate too seriously over the medium term.

Pepper cultivation

The Malaysian cultivation of pepper was first reported in Sarawak in 1856. Prior to 1980 pepper was Malaysia's third agricultural crop in terms of export earnings (after rubber and palm oil). However, since 1980, its position has deteriorated in terms of export earnings due principally to the increased Brazilian and Indonesian pepper exports. The total proceeds from the export of pepper declined from $M139.6 m. in 1977 to $M66.3 m. in 1982. The major bulk of pepper in Malaysia is still being cultivated in Sarawak. In 1984, the total Malaysian production of processed pepper was about 25 000 tonnes from about 11 000 hectares of pepper cultivation. Prices for processed pepper have generally declined since 1979; from about $M3.93 per kilo (2.2 lbs) to about $M3.26 per kilo in 1981. Since 1983, however, there has been a significant increase in the price of pepper due to a shortfall in Brazilian production. For example, the price of white pepper has increased from $M3.60 per kilo in 1982 to about $M6.50 per kilo at the end of 1983.

The world's demand for pepper has been increasing, for example the world imports of pepper increased from 155 000 tonnes in 1979 to 172 000 tonnes in 1981. In terms of Malaysian performance in the exports of pepper, up to 1979, Malaysia was the world's leading exporter of the commodity with more than 30 per cent of market share. Since 1979, its position has declined relative to that of Brazil and Indonesia: in 1983, its market share was about 22 per cent.

This declining relative world-market share of Malaysian pepper, superimposed on a generally favourable market demand conditions for pepper, implies that favourable opportunities exist for more pepper cultivation in Malaysia. Pepper cultivation is relatively capital-intensive. Its gestation period, however, is short—only two years. Based on an average white pepper price of $M7.00 per kilo, an average black pepper price of $M5.15 per kilo and normal assumptions for the cultivation costs and an economic life of ten years, the pay-back period for pepper cultivation is about three years with an internal rate of return of 30 per cent.[5] Since pepper cultivation requires relatively small land areas but a plentiful supply of labour, it is particularly suited to idle agricultural land in areas with a plentiful supply of labour and rainfall (about 100 in. per year). In the vast majority of traditional rural areas in Malaysia, such land suitable for pepper cultivation could be identified. The task remaining is to encourage the owners of such (possibly idle) land to participate in the cultivation of pepper as a cash crop.

Rubber cultivation

In 1983, Malaysia produced about 1.5 m. tonnes of natural rubber of which 0.96 m. tonnes was from smallholders and 0.55 m. tonnes from estates.[6] Out of this 1.5 m. tonnes produced, only about .06 m. tonnes was consumed locally, the remainder being exported. Thus, the viability of the rubber sector depends crucially on the world demand for natural rubber.

Since the end of the 1950s the share of natural rubber in the world elastomar market has declined from about 60 per cent in the early 1950s to about 30 per cent in the early 1970s. This is due mainly to the increasing availability of synthetic rubber. However, owing to the decreasing production cost of natural rubber and increases in the prices of petroleum leading to increasing production cost for synthetic rubber, natural rubber is expected to increase its share in the world's elastomar market in the 1980s. World natural rubber production is expected to be about 4.6 m. tonnes in 1985 and 5.0 m. tonnes by 1990 based on existing acreage and production technology; it is expected to grow at 3.8 per cent per annum between 1985–90.[7] World demand for elastomar, on the other hand, is expected to reach 16.1 m. tonnes in 1985 and 21 m. tonnes in 1990. Hence, the world natural rubber production will constitute only about 28 per cent of the world's demand for elastomar in 1985 and 24 per cent in 1990; these are low percentages by historical standard. Thus to avoid a short fall in natural rubber in the 1980s additional investments in rubber plantation are necessary. Malaysia is steadily improving its rubber production technology with the view to increase the competitiveness of its natural rubber. Recently, it has also reduced the export duty on rubber as an incentive to stimulate additional production and reinvestment.

As stated previously, extensive land resources still exist in Malaysia for new rubber cultivation. This is particularly true for investors who are willing to cooperate with the public sector or Bumiputra agencies, in the form of joint ventures for new rubber cultivation.

A factor that crucially influences the profitability of such a venture is the price of natural rubber which has fluctuated widely since the early 1980s from an average price of Malaysian 257.8 cents per kilo in 1981 to Malaysian 201.1 cents per kilo in 1982 and Malaysian 247.2 cents per kilo in 1983. A prefeasibility study for a medium-size rubber plantation (which is about 800 hectares) based on a conservative price level for natural rubber (Rubber Smoked Sheet 1) of Malaysian 200 cents/kilo and an economic life of 30 years for the rubber trees indicates that such a project has a pay-back period of an internal rate of return of 8.2 pr cent.[8] This is a fairly satisfactory rate of return, given that a rubber plantation is a very stable venture with a long period of gestation. Further, besides generating cash inflow over the duration of the project, a rubber plantation venture stands to gain substantially from the appreciation in the value of the land alienated for the plantation, or upon converting the project into another project involving an alternative use of the land such as for industrial needs or housing needs.

Aqua-culture

It is estimated that there are more than 55 000 hectares of water surface which are suitable for aqua-culture in Peninsular Malaysia alone;[9] another 150 000 hectares of mangrove swamps and mud-flats in the Peninsular are suitable for the development of aqua-culture. At the moment, only about 4 000 hectares of these swamplands are utilised mainly for the culture of cockles. Further, in the Peninsular, there are many disused mining pools which could be used for fish and other culture.

There is, therefore, considerable potential for further expansion and development for aqua-culture in Malaysia. The three main ways in which this can be developed are: (a) improvement in the operation of the existing culture systems, (b) development of new sites for existing culture systems; (c) development of new cultures suitable for the water surfaces. The main existing culture systems include:

coastal cage-culture of both *kerang* and *kerapu*
mining pool culture of freshwater fish
pond culture of marine prawns
integrated farming including duck-cum-fish rearing.

A preliminary feasibility study of each of the above culture systems[10] indicates that the pay-back period for cage-culture of *kerang* and *kerapu* is less than two years, with an internal rate of return of 45 per cent. The rate of return for freshwater fish culture in mining pools is even higher; with an internal rate of return of 125 per cent based on a one-acre abandoned mining pool. When no abandoned mining pools are available, the internal rate of return is 17 per cent based on a half-acre excavated pond. Because of the generaly higher demand for marine prawns, prawn cultivation of marine prawns is generally more profitable than pond cultivation of freshwater fish. However, the technology for prawn farming is more intricate and it is a more risky project. Nevertheless, for those with the expertise, the internal rate of return for such a project based on the construction of a suitable pond is in excess of 60 per cent with a pay-back period of less than two years.

Integrated farming based on duck-cum-fish culture is commonly practised in many other countries such as Hong Kong. In Malaysia, this has not been undertaken extensively except in some areas in Selangor, possibly because of the availability of other more attractive opportunities. Nevertheless, the feasibility study indicates that such a venture would be extremely viable in Malaysia; with an internal rate of return of 60 per cent and a pay-back period of less than two years.

Aqua-culture, on the whole, requires very little capital investment, it does however, require careful management and supervision. This is an area particularly suited to small-scale entrepreneurs interested in exploiting the economic opportunities offered by the water surfaces of the country, or to owners of fragmented agricultural land wishing to increase the productivity of their idle agricultural land.

Petroleum and gas exploration

Malaysia's history of petroleum and gas exploration started at the turn of this century. After nearly half a century of unsuccessful land exploration the search for petroleum moved off-shore with the first off-shore wells drilled in 1957. The country has a broad shallow continental shelf which occupies a significant portion of the Sunda Shelf, one of the largest continuous shallow water areas of the world. Large tracts of these off-shore areas were leased out to seven exploration companies and by the early 1970s the existence of significant pockets of oil and gas were established off-shore of Sabah, Sarawak and Trengganu. Current petroleum exploration and production are confined to the off-shore areas of these states.

The oil crisis of 1973 increased the government's awareness of the need to have control over an industry that is of vital economic and strategic importance to the nation. The 1974 Petroleum Development Act was enacted by the government, and this led to the creation of the National Petroleum Development Corporation (Petronas) as the government agency to coordinate and control the development of the petroleum industry in Malaysia. Upstream, Petronas' responsibilities are to properly manage the operation and production activities and to ensure that they are in line with the national objectives. In the first few years of operation, Petronas' role in upstream activities were limited to the supervision of the successful contractors in the exploration and production activities programmes. In 1978, however, Petronas set up a wholly-owned subsidiary, Petro Carigali, to undertake exploration and production activities in an area off the east coast of Peninsular Malaysia.

To date seven production sharing agreements are in operation: three with Esso, two with Shell, one with BP and another with Elf Aquataine. The basic features of the contracts are a 70 to 30 production split in favour of Petronas after allowing for a maximum of 20 per cent of gross production for cost recovery (25 per cent for gas) and 10 per cent of gross production for royalties. Exploration was allowed for a period of three years with a possible two-year extension. The contract areas are divided into 10-minute sub-blocks of 347 km^2 each, and when commercial oil discoveries are made, the sub-block is converted into a 'development area' with a maximum of four years being allowed for development of the field. For gas, a holding period of five years is allowed after discovery. The production phase for both oil and gas is 15 years.

The Active Exploration Programme over the period 1977–83 has resulted in a 65 per cent and a 55 per cent increase in Malaysia's oil and non-oil associated gas reserves, respectively. Total reserves in Malaysia now stand at 2.3 billion barrels of oil, 39 trillion cubic feet of non-associated gas and 10 trillion cubic feet of associated gas.[11] Although it is likely that most of the large gas and oil fields have been discovered, prospects for additional petroleum discoveries appear excellent. The deepwater areas off-shore Sabah and Sarawak are totally unexplored. However, a gas discovery was recently made off-shore Sabah from a well drilled in about 180 metres of water. The acquisition of high quality seismic data over these areas would assist in delineating sedimentary thickness and could possibly provide leads for new explorations. Further, no extensive explorations have been conducted in the Straits of Malacca. This shallow Strait could be a potential producer of oil and natural gas.

The Malaysian and Thai governments have also gazetted an eastern offshore boarder area of 7 102 sq. km as a common area for joint exploration and exploitation of hydrocarbons. This Joint Development Area is located approximately 145 km northeast of Kota Bharu and approximately 282 km east of Songkhla. Currently, negotiations are underway between Malaysia and Thailand to finalise the formal establishment of a Joint Authority which will administer the area.

Data including all existing seismic lines shot in the area and well reports have been exchanged between the two countries: seismic interpretation, geological studies and assessment of the potential hydrocarbon volumes in the area and the ranking of prospects have been carried out. The study on the economics of the area and the viability of hydrocarbon development is now in its final stages. If the results of the evaluation are affirmative this could well be another area that promises great potentials for exploration and development activities for interested investors.

Current exploration efforts have led to the discovery of 44 oil fields and 47 gas fields.[12] Twenty-three of the oil fields are producing crude oil at the rate of 444 000 barrels a day. Further, two gas fields are in production, with output averaging 500 m. cubic feet per day. Figure 8.1 shows the oil and gas fields being currently explored in Malaysia. In monetary terms, investment in the exploration and production of petroleum is expected to reach $M2.9 billion in 1984.

The types of crude produced from the current oil fields are Tapis, Tembungo, Labuan, Miri and Bintulu. Malaysian crude is of premium quality and fetches higher prices than Arabian light, the marker crude.

The discovery of significant gas reserves besides oil has enabled the country to become a significant exporter of Liquefied Natural Gas (LNG) and prompted the country to promote the use of gas as an alternative source of energy supply.

The Bintulu-LNG Plant was constructed at a cost of $M3.6 billion and was commissioned in 1984; its initial shipment of LNG to Japan was completed in March 1984. In Trengganu, a gas processing plant and a petrochemical complex using gas as the feedstock have been planned. Similarly in Sabah, two heavy industrial projects, a methanol plant and a sponged iron plant using natural gas as feedstock and fuel respectively, have been planned.

Domestically, the market for natural gas seems promising. Petronas has embarked on the implementation of the LNG pipeline reticulation scheme and the natural gas distribution system.

Investment opportunities in manufacturing

Malaysia has an ambitious industrial vision of achieving the status of an advanced Newly Industrialised Country (NIC) by 1990. In the top tier of Malaysia's industrialisation goal comes the energy development programme which aims at extracting and processing the vast reserves of oil and gas in the east coast of Peninsular Malaysia, Sabah and Sarawak. The gas and oil pipeline projects linking Trengganu's off-shore oil field with Kerteh, the methol and ammonia plants in Telok Kalong, and the Bintulu LNG plant are some of the projects under this top category. In the second tier is the proposed petro-

Figure 8.1 Oil and gas fields in Malaysia

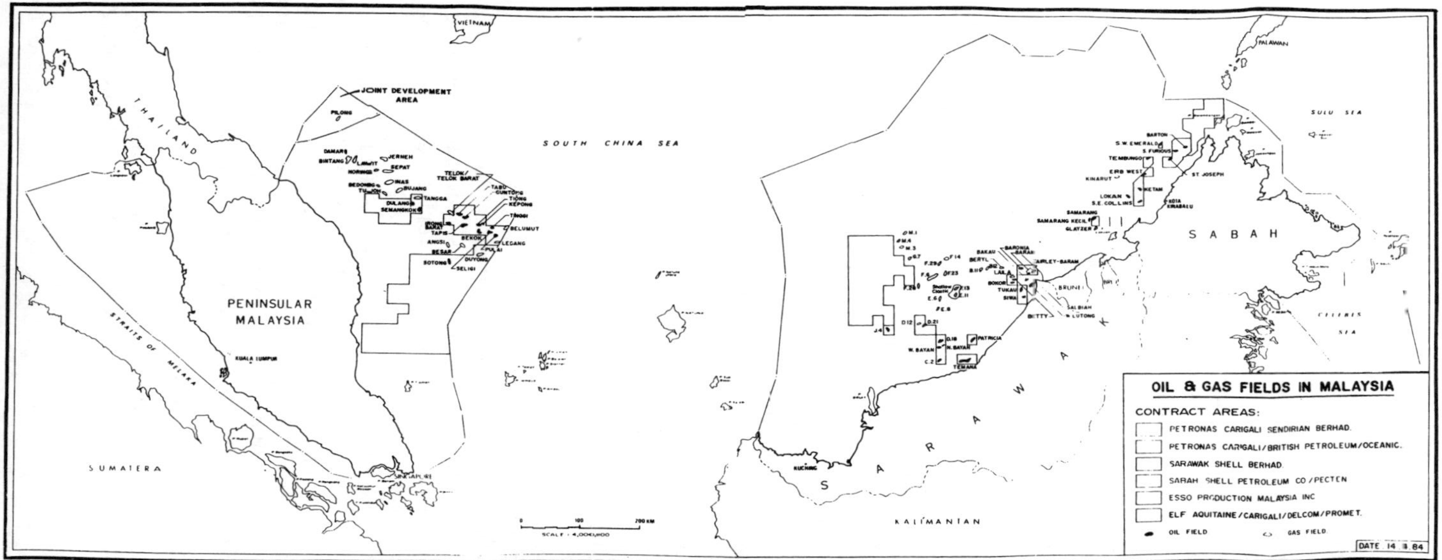

chemical complex in Trengganu which seeks to produce up-stream industrial petrochemical raw materials (like ethylene, High Density Polyethylene and Low Density Polyethylene) using natural gas as feedstocks. Next comes other heavy industries such as the Trengganu integrated steel mill and the Labuan sponge iron plant using, again, mainly natural gas as the fuel source and the made-in Malaysia car project. It is hoped that with the establishment of the petrochemical plant and the heavy industries, sufficient local industrial raw materials could be manufactured to encourage the development of more light and medium industries. Since these light and medium industries are then based on locally produced raw materials, they could potentially be extremely competitive in the world market. If the establishment of the petrochemical complex, the two iron and steel projects and the Malaysian car project could lead to the achievement of this fourth tier (which is the development of high quality, and competitive, light and medium industries such as plastics, textiles and component manufacturing), then the heavy investment incurred by these extremely capital intensive projects could be justified. Finally, in the fifth tier, with the successful establishment of light and medium industries, it is hoped that a whole range of resource-based industries, like wood-based and rubber-based industries, could then be efficiently developed to further deepen the Malaysian industrial sector.

The Malaysian industrial vision is then the existence of a thriving and vast industrial sector, based on locally produced industrial inputs, and producing both light and medium industrial goods competitively in the world market. The petrochemical and heavy industries development programme is but a catalyst, albeit a very important one, in the whole process. The heavy investment committed to this programme represents really the premium the country has to pay to launch itself onto the path of being a advanced NIC by 1990. Given its resources of oil and gas, this path seems to be very prudent, although not without risks. It is the prudent path, for otherwise the country would continue to be stagnant and remain as mere suppliers of raw materials, including oil and gas, to the advanced countries. Malaysia has remained far too long a supplier of raw materials. This is the right time for it to fulfil its industrial vision and take the more risky path of upgrading its industrial technological level, and deepening its industrial sector, to a level consistent with the other advanced NICs. This strategy of governmental intervention in industrialisation provides numerous opportunities for the private sector to participate in the rapidly expanding industrial sector. Some of these opportunities are elaborated below.

Resource-based industries

In the area of *rubber-based industries* a major emphasis of the government is to promote Malaysia as a major producer and exporter of *automobile tyres*. Although Malaysia is the major producer of natural rubber only three tyre companies operate in the country —namely Goodyear, Dunlop and IT International. These companies produce tyres mainly for the domestic market.

Over the period 1978–83 there has been a decline in the value of tyres exported; from $M20 m. in 1978 to only $M8.8 m. in 1983. This decline in export value was experienced notwithstanding the fact that the ex-factory sales of tyres within the country has increased from $M177 m. in 1978 to $M323 m. in 1983.[13] This could be due to the increasing competition experienced by Malaysian tyre manufacturers in the world market.

A demand analysis for tyres, conducted by Smit (1982)[14] and by the Malaysia Rubber Task Force on the natural rubber industry, anticipates a gradual recovery in both original equipment and replacement market for tyres. It is anticipated that the export market for tyres will then increase and the export of Malaysian tyres will expand in line with the trend established in the 1970s.

However, the world tyre market is extremely competitive, for Malaysia to emerge as a major exporter of tyres it will have to attract prominent international tyre manufacturers utilising the most modern tyre manufacturing technologies. The Malaysian government is committed to provide generous incentive to these manufacturers and in its 1984 budget additional protection and tariffs have been granted for the tyre industry in Malaysia. If these incentives can lead to the establishment of more multi-national subsidiaries or joint ventures based on the latest technologies, and the tyres manufactured can be re-exported through the parent company's marketing channels there is no reason why Malaysia could not emerge as a successful major producer of tyres, bringing benefits to both the multi-national corporations and the domestic economy. Interviews with existing rubber industrialists in Malaysia indicate that with the new protection, additional incentives, and possible domestic availability of synthetic rubber, Malaysia represents a potentially competitive environment for the manufacture of tyres, particularly specialised tyres such as those for aircrafts and heavy movers.

Besides tyre production, the government is also providing incentives for the manufacturing of other rubber-based items such as *rubber gloves, rubber foam mattresses* and *rubber domestic apparels.* These items are most appropriate for small ancillary units, and would be particularly attractive to domestic investors.

The second major class of resource-based industries suitable for the country are those based on *palm oil*. Palm oil represents a close substitute to animal fats and can be processed into various items such as *fatty acids*, *margarine*, *cooking oil*, *oil-base* for pharmaceutical products, *industrial margarine* for bakeries and confectioneries, *vegetable shortening* and non-edible uses such as *soap* and oil-base for industrial processes. To make these items the crude palm oil (extracted from the palm oil fruit bunches) must be refined and processed into its secondary products of olein and stearin. A feasibility study undertaken,[15] based on current world demand for vegetable oils and fats, showed that the internal rate of return for such a project is 15 per cent using the dry fractional process with a capacity of 50 tonnes per day and a crude palm oil of $M850 per tonne. The net present value (at 12 per cent discount rate) of the project is $M0.7 m. The project's pay-back period is about 3.6 years.

Given that palm oil is the fastest growing agricultural subsector in the country and the government intends promoting more extensive secondary processing of palm oil, the future for palm oil processing activities seems bright. At present there are about 64 palm oil refineries in Peninsular Malaysia producing crude palm oil mainly for export for further refining and processing. The bulk of this crude palm oil could be refined and processed further, within the country, before being exported.

Another major class of resource-based activities promoted by the government are those based on extensive use of tropical hardwood for producing products such as *plywood*, *veneer* and *fabricated furniture*. Although Malaysia is one of the world's major exporters of logs and sawn timber its export performance in secondary wood products has been disappointing. For example in 1983, the total value of plywood exported was $M245 m. in comparison with $M1 280 m. worth of sawn timber exported. In 1980, in Peninsular Malaysia, there were a total of 650 sawmills but only 35 veneer and plywood factories.[16] Similarly, in Sabah, a major timber producing state, in 1980 there were a total of 214 sawmills but only 7 veneer and plywood factories; in Sarawak, there were a total of 34 sawmills but only 4 veneer and plywood factories. These figures indicate the tremendous scope that exists in the country for the production of secondary wood products. With the government's intention to ban all exports of logs by 1985, and the recovery of the world economy leading to an increase in demand for secondary wood products, these activities are potentially viable industrial activities in Malaysia. The technology required for these processes is relatively simple and the country, with its wide base of sawmills, has a ready supply of skilled labour for these secondary wood processing plants.

The main problems facing the potential investors would be the wide variability in the price of timber and the identification of proper channels through which the products could be exported. Investment in secondary wood-processing plants would be particularly attractive to existing large Japanese and Korean furniture manufacturers faced with a shortage in the supply of logs and increasing labour costs in their home environments. Existing sawmills in the country should also consider upgrading their scope of activities to include secondary processing to increase their profitability and diversify their total dependence on export of sawn timber.

Another major group of resource-based industries that have scope in the country are those products based on *petroleum* and *natural gas* which are being produced off-shore in Trengganu, Sabah and Sarawak. The Malaysian government is proposing an ambitious petrochemical development programme which involves the processing of natural gas, the conversion of the treated natural gas into ethylene, propylene and polyethylene. This programme has already been described previously and is presented in greater detail in table 8.2. In particular, the petrochemical complex is expected to come on stream in the late 1980s. With the availability of the basic petrochemicals, extensive opportunities exist for interested entrepreneurs to utilise the produced basic petrochemicals as inputs for the production of downstream petrochemicals such as *PVC*, *polysterine* and *plastic products*. In particular, production of high quality plastic products for both the domestic and the world market appears to be a viable venture, given the availability of domestic raw materials.

High-tech industries

The govenment is emphasising the production of high-tech industries such as electronic components, computers and capital goods industry as well as resource-based industries.

The electronics assembly plants have formed the backbone of the Malaysian industrialisation drive since the 1970s and by 1980, Malaysia had become the world's major exporter of integrated circuits with a total export value of $M2 604 m; the majority of these are produced by the electronics-component assembly plants established in the various free trade zones in the 1970s with pioneer status. However, the majority of these plants are now approaching the end of their tax-free periods. Many of these plants are now re-negotiating with the government for extension of these tax-free periods. Against this backdrop and against the rising wage and labour-shortage trends of the country, greater emphasis is now being given by the government towards encouraging these electronics-component assembly plants to upgrade their assembly operations into *wafer fabrication plants*. This represents an upgrading of the present labour-intensive electronics assembly operation, and is the logical development of the Malaysian electronics industry.

Another area of potential investment in the electronics industry is the production of consumer electronics items such as *televisions*, *radios*, *digital clocks*, *watches* and *electronic musical instruments*. The major thrust of Malaysia's electronics industrialisation drive has been over-emphasis of the production of integrated circuits for the world markets. There has been neglect of production of electronics

Table 8.2 Proposed Malaysian petrochemical development programme

Project	Capacity	Completion date	Cost ($Mm.)	Manpower	Natural gas consumption	Location
Off-shore gas pipeline	104 miles 30″ Submarine trunkline of capacity 400 mscf/d	1984	720	na	—	Kerteh, Trengganu
Gas processing plant	130 mscf/d (1984) 400 mscf/d (1987) Extraction of ethane, propane and butane and their condensation; also LNG	1984	132	70	130 mscf/d (1984) 400 mscf/d (1987)	Kerteh, Trengganu
Ammonia/urea plant (ASEAN project)	360 (Ammonia) 540 (Urea)	1984	781	360	Treated natural gas (40–80 mscf/d)	Bintulu, Sarawak
Petrochemical complex	Ethylene (200) Propylene (20–40) HDPE (85) LDPE (120)	Not Decided	2 100	200	Ethane (285) Treated natural gas (as fuel)	Kerteh, Trengganu
Ammonia plant	450	1987	770	470	Treated natural gas (40 mscf/d)	Kerteh or Telok Kalong, Trengganu
Methol plant	450	1987	520	130	Treated natural gas (45 mscf/d)	Telok Kalong, Trengganu

Source: Kuala Lumpur: Petronas, 1982
Notes: Mscf/d denotes million standard cubic feet per day
All other unspecified units are in thousand tonnes per year

consumer durables for the export and domestic markets. Production of electronics consumer durables is a particularly good opportunity for domestic entrepreneurs who may wish to acquire the necessary equipment from foreign sources to start up such plants. Technology for the manufacture of these items is relatively well-developed and many foreign equipment suppliers would be willing to provide the necessary technology for such processes.

Based on the country's desire to diversify its industrial base and to strengthen its self-reliance on the *capital goods* industry, substantial opportunities exist for plants seeking to produce components and parts for the engineering industries, the heavy industries, as well as for the Malaysian car project. Since these component-producing plants should ideally be small ancillary units, they are suited for domestic entrepreneurs interested in the setting up of modern ancillary units. Further, substantial opportunities also exist for the production of capital goods such as lathes, drills and other capital goods required by many of Malaysia's new plants. The government is seriously considering the implementation of a second round of import substitution aimed at encouraging the establishment of a viable capital goods industry in the country. Concrete plans are now (mid-1985) being formalised and the details of these plans will be announced now.

Investment opportunities in the services sector

Rapid industrialisation and rapid increase in income levels would induce a significant expansion of the services sector over the next decade. Opportunities in the services sector are some of the most profitable investment opportunities in the country. A major growth area in the service sector is the *tourist sector*. Among ASEAN countries, the Malaysian tourist sector is, next to Indonesia, the least developed. This is notwithstanding the fact that the country possesses numerous historical and tourist attractions, such as the tourist island of Penang, the historic site of Malacca, and the numerous scenic spots in Sabah and Sarawak. With the deterioration of the balance of payments in the services account since the early 1980s, the government is taking bold steps to encourage a revitalisation of the tourist sector. Most hotels built in the country can be offered pioneer status. In 1984, these incentives were extended to include traditional lower-quality hotels which wish to upgrade their facilities into suitable business and tourist hotels. Although numerous new hotels have been constructed in Kuala Lumpur and Petaling Jaya, this has not been the case in other first-rate tourist centres such as Malacca, Port Dickson, Kuching and Kota Kinabalu. Investment in hotels in these relatively unexploited tourist centres represents potentially viable investment opportunities for the domestic as well as foreign investors.

A major problem that needs to be overcome by interested investors in hotels is the linking up of their facilities to some of the well-known hotel chains. This is to ensure a steady in-flow of guest arrivals to these hotels. Given the increasing government emphasis on encouraging the local tour agencies to promote Malaysia as a tourist destination, these entrepreneurs should cooperate with the tour agencies to ensure a steady tourist arrival rate. A preliminary feasibility study[17] of a tourist hotel complex in Malacca indicates that the internal rate of return of such a project, based on an occupancy rate of 60 per cent, would be around 20 per cent. This is a reasonable rate of return, given the large economic link of the project to the local economy.

Another major growth area in the services sector is *private higher education centres* preparing students for external examinations such as the 'O' and 'A' levels, the Association of Certified Chartered Accountant (ACCA), London Chamber of Commerce Institute (LCCI) and London City and Guilds Examination, as well as offering the equivalent of the first two years of a USA undergraduate degree. The demand for higher education in Malaysia is almost insatiable. In 1984, it was estimated that there were 50 000 Malaysian students studying in various countries overseas. In order to rectify the balance of payments' problem created by the out-flow of fees and cost-of-living payments, the government is encouraging the establishment of more private centres which could cater for the first two years of a student's college education in Malaysia, before these students are sent overseas to pursue the final two years of their college education. For educators this represents a golden opportunity in which they can contribute their services. Two such colleges, the Petaling Jaya Community College and the Damansara Utama College, have already been established. Substantial opportunities still exist for more such colleges to be established.

Another growth area in the services' sector is the establishment of *private medical centres*. With increasing affluence the demand for good quality private medical services has been on the increase and every year many Malaysian patients go overseas for medical treatment because the needed treatments are either not available or, if available, are subjected to long waiting periods in Malaysia. At present there are only a few private medical centres including the Pantai Medical Centre in Kuala Lumpur, the Assunta Hospital in Petaling Jaya, the Penang Specialist Centre and the Ipoh Specialist Centre. More such centres could be established in the other major urban areas. The government is actively encouraging the privatisation of the health services and has already started with the privatisation of the well-known Lady Templer Hospital with a group of private practitioners.

Another area of opportunity in the services' sector is *retailing* and *franchising*, especially in fast food. With increasing affluence, fast food is rapidly gaining a strong foothold in Malaysia with a total of 53 such fast food outlets: 30 Kentucky Fried Chicken outlets, 14 A&W outlets, 5 outlets for McDonald's and 4 outlets for Wendy's. Although no official statistics are available it is estimated that the 1982 turnover for fast food was about $M150 m.,[18] with a growth rate of about 10 to 20 per cent per annum. The Kentucky Fried Chicken's outlet in Sungai Wang Plaza in Kuala Lumpur is reportedly grossing about $M30 000 in sales daily. Overall, Kentucky Fried Chicken's annual turnover in the country is about $M70 m.

The major thrust of the fast food outlets in Malaysia has been in Kuala Lumpur and Petaling Jaya. Industrial sources estimate that Penang and Johore Bahru represent the next potential cities which are ready for the onslaught of fast food business. From experiences of previous successful fast food chains, the major criteria that can determine the viability of a fast food chain include the pedestrian traffic close to the outlet, the value-for-money of the foods served and the reliability of the services offered. Thus, Kentucky Fried Chicken has been very successful because it has located the majority of its outlets in busy shopping areas. Its services have also been consistent and are regarded as being very good in relation to its prices. Further, its product, chicken, is acceptable to all the major religious groups in the country. Another successful chain, the McDonald's, has established all its outlets in extremely high traffic areas. It has also emphasised on a product which provides value for money.

Recently the fast food subsector has grown tremendously but it is by no means saturated. It is a risky business but for those with a well-developed strategy and the necessary capital this could be a very lucrative business.

General retailing also represents a good investment opportunity in the country. Since 1980, a large number of department stores, with either domestic or foreign majority interests, have been established in the country. These include Metrojaya, Klasse Department Store, Kimisawa and Printemps. The experiences of these retail outlets have exceeded the investors' initial wildest expectations.

The experiences of Printemps and Kimisawa are good cases in point. Established in a previously isolated part of Petaling Jaya, they were not initially given strong chances of success. However with extensive lines of high quality merchandise and sound marketing strategies, since opening in late 1983, these retailing outlets are reported to be doing extremely well. This is manifested by the constant long queues of cars waiting for parking spaces in these outlets.

Can equally successful outlets be established in other similar suburbs in Kuala Lumpur and other metropolitan centres? The

a manifestation of success in the car parking franchise business answers to these questions lies in: (i) the management expertise of the outlet (ii) the range of merchandise provided by the outlet (iii) the general value for money of the services provided. If experiences of past successful retailing outlets in Kuala Lumpur are a guide, for a well-managed outlet, the return on investment appears to be extraordinarily high.

Investment opportunities in the construction sector

The construction sector is another high growth opportunity in the services' sector. Investments in public infrastructural projects represent one of the main accelerators of the economy. Under the Fourth Malaysian Plan a total of $M9 290 m. will be spent by the government on these projects. Any visitor to Kuala Lumpur would realise the vast range of construction activities being undertaken in the city, ranging from high-rise buildings to roads, bridges and other facilities. The bulk of public and private infrastructural projects have been undertaken by foreign construction firms, particularly those from Korea and Japan. With the emphasis of the government in encouraging local participation in the construction sector and transfer of technology from the foreign to the domestic construction sector, substantial opportunities appear to exist in the country for construction related activities, utilising domestic construction firms. Those local firms which have fulfilled the conditions of the NEP would be given special preference by the government in its tendering process.

In the construction sector housing and industrial building construction is another major area of development. With a large young population there is a great demand for housing, particularly single-storeyed and double-storeyed link houses. Developers who ventured into this business have been known to make good profits in a relatively short time. Unfortunately government regulations governing the development of housing estates are extremely tight and the approval procedure is slow. However for investors who have the patience to see the process through the financial rewards have been well worthwhile.

A major problem confronting the domestic construction firms has been their inability to compete with the international construction firms on the basis of price and production technology. In this respect, the government would have to continue to depend on the active participation of the foreign construction firms. However it is prudent for those successful foreign firms to have extensive training programmes that would ensure the rapid transfer of technology to their domestic counterparts. The upgrading of the technical ability of their domestic construction partners would ensure more meaningful, stable and rewarding relationships between the domestic and foreign partners in the numerous opportunities available to them in the rapidly growing economy of Malaysia.

9

Starting a business in Malaysia

Thusfar I have discussed in considerable detail the structure of the Malaysian economy, the financial and marketing systems, and the business opportunities that exist therein. For investors, businessmen and entrepreneurs interested in participating in the opportunities that exist in the rapidly industrialising Malaysia, I provide a summary here of the steps one can take. For interested investors I detail how to form a business enterprise, ranging from the incorporation of a suitable business enterprise, the tax environment, the sources of funds for the investment and the employment policies for the new venture. At the close of this chapter, I have also included a directory of useful contacts: relevant government agencies and statutory authorities and the various trade associations and other bodies that could provide further information to interested investors.

Methods of conducting business

In Malaysia a business enterprise may be established in any one of the following forms:

a sole proprietorship
a partnership (of 2 to 20 partners)
a corporation.

Sole proprietorship

This form of business is operated solely by an individual who is responsible for the entire business. All sole proprietorships must register with the Registrar of Business under the Registration of Business Ordinance, 1956.

Partnership

In an ordinary partnership all partners have unlimited liability for the debts and obligations of the partnership if assets are found to be insufficient. In partnerships contracted with 'inactive [sleeping] partners', the liability of at least one of the partners must be unlimited. Partnership businesses, like the sole proprietorship, are to be registered with the Registrar of Business.

Corporation

The incorporation of companies as well as the regulation of some details of their operation (including the manner in which they borrow funds), are governed by the Companies Act, 1965. Local and foreign investors who wish to incorporate a company in Malaysia must register with the Registrar of Companies under the Ministry of Trade and Industry.

According to the Act, any two or more persons may form an incorporated company. Exchange control permission is not required for direct investments by non-residents. The non-residents themselves and Registrar of Companies are responsible for ensuring compliance with the conditions set by the Ministry of Trade and Industry regarding capital participation.

There are four different types of companies which can be incorporated:

company limited by shares
company limited by guarantee
company limited both by shares and guarantee and
unlimited company.

'Company limited by shares' is a company where the liability of its members confines only to the amount (if any) of the unpaid shares owned by them as stated in the Memorandum of Association. In a 'company limited by guarantee', the liability of members in the event of dissolution or liquidation is restricted to the amount each agrees to contribute to the assets of the company.

Generally, the first type of company would be of more interest to overseas organisations or investors for it can be either a private or a public company.

Private limited companies

A company having a share capital may be corporated as a private company if its Memorandum or Article, first, restricts the right to transfer its shares; second, limits the number of its members to 50 (excluding employees and some former employees); third, prohibits any invitation to the public to subscribe for its shares and the debentures; and fourthly, prohibits any invitation to the public to deposit money with the company.

Public companies

A company can be formed as a public company or alternatively, a company which is incorporated as a private company can also be converted to a public company subject to Section 26 of the Companies Act, 1965.

A public company cannot offer shares to the public unless a prospectus which complies with the requirement of the Companies Act has been registered with the Registrar of Companies. The prospectus will also need to be approved by the Capital Issues Committee.

A public company can apply to the KLSE for permission to have its shares quoted on the Exchange. This is, however, subject to the compliance with the requirements laid down by the KLSE.

Procedures for incorporation of companies

Investors wishing to establish a business in Malaysia are invited to contact MIDA (Malaysia Industrial Development Authority). From the first letter of inquiry through the process of setting up a manufacturing company, MIDA serves as the central agency from which all information on industry may be obtained to assist investors in making the right decisions.

It is the policy of the Malaysian government to welcome foreign investment in industries in the country on a joint-venture basis with local Malaysian investors. As an organisation set up with the dual objective of promoting and coordinating industrial development in Malaysia, MIDA will undertake to give whatever assistance possible in the establishment of such industrial joint-venture projects. The establishment of the Registry of Potential Investors represents part of MIDA's efforts towards this direction, and it is hoped that this will result in more joint-venture projects being incorporated.

The following are the procedures to be followed for the incorporation of a private company and public company in Malaysia:

Private company

1 Inquire from the Registrar of Companies if the proposed name of the intended company is acceptable for registration. Information on the business and type of company should be given. A search fee of $M5.00 should be paid to the Registrar.

2 If the name of the intended company is acceptable, apply for reservation of the name on Form 14 (in duplicate). The filing

fee is $M15.00. The proposed name will be reserved by the Registrar for two months from the date of reservation. A fee of $M5.00 has to be paid for any extention after the two months. However, reservation of a name does not in itself entitle the intended company to be registered by that name.

3 Once the name has been reserved, the Memorandum and Articles of Association should be lodged with the Registrar of Companies. The Memorandum of Association is the document stating the name, objectives, the amount of authorised capital (if any) with which the company proposed to register and the division thereof into shares of a fixed amount. The Articles of Association are the regulations governing the internal management of the affairs of the company and the operation of its business.

4 Submit the following documents to the Registrar of Companies:

Form 6	— Statutory declaration of Compliance by a Director or a Secretary of the Company
Form 7	— Certificate of Identity in respect of the subscribers to and officers named in Memorandum of Association
Form 24	— Allotment of Shares Return
Form 44	— Notice of Situation of Registered Office
Form 45	— Consent to Act as Director
Form 48A	— Statutory Declaration by a Person before Appointment as Director, or by a Promoter before Incorporation, to be signed before the Commissioner for Oaths; and
Form 49	— Data about Directors, Managers and Secretary

Filling fees for the aforementioned documents are $M5.00 each except for Form 48A, whose filing fee is $M10.00. The filing fees for the Memorandum and Articles of Association are $M10.00 for the original copy and $M2.00 for the duplicate. The total registration fees for companies with specific amounts of authorised capital are shown in appendix 5.

5 On approval of the registration of the company, obtain a Certificate of Incorporation from the Registrar of Companies. Obtain also the seal, registers and forms of share certificates.

6 Prepare the agenda for the first board meeting.

7 Where the Forms 24, 44 and 49 have not been lodged with the Registrar in accordance with step 4 above, these shall have to be lodged with the Registrar within one month after the date of incorporation of the company.

Public company

The procedure for incorporation of a public company follows the steps of that for a private limited company up to the stage when the Certificate of Incorporation is issued. However, a public company cannot commence business until an indication by the Registrar through a certificate as provided under Section 52 of the Companies Act.

General

If the business of the intended company is to be conducted in East Malaysia (Sabah or Sarawak), it should obtain a business registration in the state concerned apart from having itself incorporated.

Requirements of a locally incorporated company

The procedures for the incorporation of a company described so far refer or apply to a locally incorporated company, and have to conform to the requirements below:

1 It must have a registered office in Malaysia where the registers and documents required by statute should be kept.
2 A company cannot deal with its own shares or hold shares in its holding company. Each equity share of a public company carries only one vote at a poll at any general meeting. A private company may, however, provide for varying voting rights for its shareholders.
3 The company secretary and at least two of its directors must have their place of residence in Malaysia. Director of public companies must not exceed 70 years of age. It is not incumbent that director should also be a shareholder.
4 The auditors must be approved company auditors in Malaysia.
5 The company is required to hold its First Annual General Meeting within 18 months after incorporation and subsequently once every calendar year and lay the annual accounts before the members thereat.

Establishment of a foreign branch operation

A foreign incorporated company may establish and operate a subsidiary company or branch in Malaysia to carry on business of its parent-company. Application for registration must be made to the Registrar of Companies, subject to the approval of the Domestic Trade Division, Ministry of Trade and Industry. When the approval has been obtained such a branch must lodge with the Registrar of Companies the following documents:

1 A certified copy of its Certificate of Incorporation (or document of similar effect);
2 A certified copy of its charter statute on Memorandum and Articles of Association (or other instrument defining its constitution);
3 A list of its directors and certain statutory particulars regarding them;
4 Where there are local directors, a memorandum stating the powers of those directors;
5 A memorandum of appointment of power of attorney authorising person(s) residing in Malaysia to accept, on behalf of the company, service of process and any notice required to be served on the company;
6 Notice of the situation of its Registered Office in Malaysia and the working hours; and
7 A statutory declaration in the prescribed form made by the agent of the company.

The appointed agent is answerable for the performance of all acts required to be done by the company under the Companies Act, 1965. Any changes in agents must be reported to the Registrar of Companies.

A foreign incorporated company must file annually, within two months of its Annual General Meeting, a copy of the balance sheet of its head office, audited profit and loss accounts, and a duly audited balance sheet of its operations in Malaysia.

The fees payable for lodging the various forms as well as the fees for registration of a foreign company can be made to the Registrar of Companies.

Procedure for application of an industrial licence

The Industrial Coordination Act, which was enforced by the Malaysian government on 1 May 1976, requires a licence for all business and manufacturing activities, whether for existing projects, expansion of projects or new proposals. However, industrial projects which employ less than 25 full-time paid employees or have a capital of less than $M250 000, producers of crude palm oil, Standard Malaysian Rubber (SMR), Rubber Smoked Sheet (RSS) and Crepe Rubber are also exempted from licensing provision.

The prescribed application form for a licence must be filled and submitted to the Ministry of Trade and Industry through MIDA. An application may be made for one or more products manufactured in one or more places of manufacturing activity, but for each place of manufacturing activity a separate licence will be issued.

Procedure for applying for manufacturing licence under the Industrial Coordination Act, 1975

The following explains the procedures for applying for a licence to carry out any manufacturing activity or business in Malaysia:

1 Applications should be submitted in accordance with Forms ICA (1 to 5) prescribed under the Industrial Coordination Act, 1975.

2 Firms or persons who need to apply for manufacturing licence under the Industrial Coordination Act, 1975 can be categorised as follows:

  a Manufacturers who have received approval, with or without incentives, from the Ministry of Trade and Industry before the coming into force of the Act;

  b Existing manufacturers who have not received approval from the Ministry of Trade and Industry before the coming into force of the Act;

  c Firms or persons who intend to establish manufacturing industries after the date of enforcement of the Act; and

  d Existing manufacturers intending to undertake expansion of existing capacities or to manufacture additional products.

3 Applicants are required to submit 15 copies of their applications to MIDA. Applicants from Sabah and Sarawak, besides sending 15 copies as prescribed above. 3 extra copies of the applications to the authority of the state concerned.

4 The fee to be paid under Section 4 of the Industrial Coordination Act, 1975 is $M50.00 for each manufacturing licence issued. This will be a once-and-for all payment for licences issued to manufactures in categories (a) to (c) of paragraph 3 above and this payment should be made at the time of issuance of licence. Firms or persons (under Category (d)) will also be charged a fee $M50.00 each time their original licence is modified to include additional products approved. A fee of $M50.00 per copy will also be charged for duplicates or replacement of licences.

5 Where the manufacturing projects proposed require the conclusion of agreements pertaining to technical know-how, marginal expertise, patents, trade marks, marketing and other matters for the implementation of the projects, 3 copies of the agreement are required to be submitted to the Industries Division of the Ministry of Trade and Industry for approval. If the actual draft agreements are not available at the time of submission of

the application form, a summary of the main provisions of the proposed agreements should be submitted.

Sources of financing

Investors who locate their industrial projects or incorporate their business in Malaysia will find a variety of financing instruments easily available. Besides accessibility to such facilities, they are also ensured of a modern and efficient banking system which is comparable with those offered by international financial centres. Among the more important financing institutions are the commercial banks, finance companies, the merchant banks and discount houses.

Commercial banks

Commercial banking is well developed in Malaysia. They are the most important local source of financing. They provide normal banking services such as accepting deposits, making loans and advances, discounting trade bills, dealing in foreign exchange and also providing business investment advisory services. Besides that, commercial banks also accept deposits, including demand deposits for the smooth functioning of the payments mechanism in the country, fixed deposits of maturity periods of one to 60 months, saving deposits and negotiable certificates of deposit.

To broaden the commercial banks funding base, they are permitted to undertake foreign borrowing. To facilitate this development, the commercial banks are also allowed to lend and syndicate loans in foreign currency to residents for productive purposes and to finance the buying of assets in Malaysia owned by non-residents. Commercial bank lending is channelled to various sectors of the economy, with the banks also being called upon to lend to specific priority sectors of the economy. The role of commercial banks in the economic development of the country has become increasingly important. As the Malaysian economy moves progressively towards resource-based and heavy industries, measures have been undertaken to improve and promote a sound banking structure to raise the capability of the commercial banking system to meet the increasing financial needs of the economy.

Finance companies

The second largest mobilisers of deposit funds in the country are the finance companies. The finance companies are also the second most important institutional source of private sector credit after the commercial banks. These finance companies operate in the short-to-medium term credit market, but they are not allowed to accept demand deposit and granting loans in the form of overdrafts and unsecured loans of more than $M5 000. However, they offer savings and fixed deposit facilities and normally pay higher interest rates as compare with commercial banking. Credit extended by the finance companies comprised mainly hire-purchase loans, leasing finance, housing loans and short to medium-term loans for business and private purposes.

Merchant banks

The merchant banks have a role in helping to promote new investment (including foreign investment) in the country to sustain the growth of domestic productive capacity. It is because of their widespread network of international banking contacts and foreign shareholders and their indepth knowledge of domestic markets and corporate needs.

Merchant banks operate mainly in wholesale banking and a full range of specialised financial services relating to all aspects of corporate financing, financial investment and management advice, and investment portfolio management, including services for the structuring of ownership and the upgrading of financial management in the corporate and public enterprise sector.

To broaden their funding base in order to service industry more effectively, the merchant banks are permitted (since 1982), to accept deposits denominated in foreign currency from non-residents. Further, they are also permitted to grant loans in foreign currency to assist in the financing of the building of new domestic productive capacity and the purchase of assets in Malaysia. The merchant banks too are permitted to invest in corporate equity to provide 'venture capital' or 'seed money' to assist in the growth of enterprising businesses or new industrial ventures. In the aggregate, a merchant bank may invest in shares valued up to a total of 25 per cent of its paid-up capital and published shares. In short, merchant banks act not only as banking instruments but more importantly, as capital raising to business enterprises.

Leasing companies

Leasing, though relatively new to Malaysia has, nevertheless, provided industrialists with another form of financial facility. Currently, there are 60 companies engaged either partly or wholly in leasing (Malaysia, 1984).

In the 1982 budget, the Malaysian government announced an 100 per cent accelerated depreciation allowance (ADA) to be applied to leased equipment. In addition to this tax consideration, advantages in leasing include improved liquidity, freeing of working capital and the development of capital for other productive uses.

Bank Negara Malaysia

Bank Negara Malaysia is the Central Bank of Malaysia. The principal objectives of the bank are to issue currency and to keep reserves, safeguarding the value of the currency; to act as banker and financial adviser to the government; to promote monetary stability and sound financial structure; and to influence the credit situation to the advantage of the country. Its other functions include acting as agent for raising and managing internal and external loans, carrying out credit operations with the banking system as a lender of last resort, including discounting and discounting bills, operating in foreign exchange and administering exchange control regulations.

Malaysia Industrial Development Finance Berhad (MIDF)

The next financing institution which an investor can look for is the MIDF. The MIDF was incorporated in 1960 as a private company and was restructured in 1963 as a public company with the participation of Malaysian company and the World Bank. The principal aim of MIDA is to promote rapid industrial growth in Malaysia by providing the assistance to both the local and foreign entrepreneurs in establishing sound industrial enterprise.

The company covers a wide spectrum of activities, including the provision of medium and long-term finance, underwriting, management of consortium loans with commercial banks and financial and managerial advice to entrepreneurs. Under certain circumstances MIDF may also assist by subscribing to the shares of the client companies. This equity will be relinquished as soon as the market conditions warrant while ensuring that the client's interest is protected.

Malaysia Export Credit Insurance Berhad (MECIB)

The establishment of the MECIB in 1979 by the Malaysian government was aimed to promote the export of manufactured goods, and to provide exporters of manufactured products with export credit insurance. It is the government's policy to stimulate and diversify, more export-led industrialisation in the country.

For short-term goods or services requiring payment terms not more than 180 days, MECIB offers the Comprehensive Whole Turnover Shipments/Contracts or Services Rendered Policies. These cover up to 85 per cent of any loss that may be incurred by the exporters.

In addition, MECIB provides Pre-shipment or Post-shipment Bank Guarantees for the purpose of export financing. Medium or long-term buyer credit or supplier credit under Specific Bank Guarantee can also be arranged.

Recruitment of labour

The labour and manpower profile and supply in Malaysia has been discussed in depth in chapter 5, and also the recruitment policies. Malaysia's youthful labour force which is diligent, disciplined, plentiful and readily trainable, has been regarded as one of its most important natural resources. Many of them also possess the basic skills required by industries. Furthermore, there is an increasing supply of professionals, technologists and other middle and lower-level skilled workers graduating from the local universities, colleges and other technical and industrial training institutions in the country.

Employment of expatriate personnel

It is the Malaysian government's policy to see that Malaysians are eventually trained and employed at all levels of employment. Foreign companies, however, are allowed to recruit foreign personnel in areas where there is a shortage of trained Malaysians to do the job, and for certain 'key posts' permanently to safeguard their interests.

The principal elements guiding the government in its consideration of expatriate posts are:

1 Key post (a post that can be held indefinitely by foreigners) can be considered for companies with foreign capital participation of approximately $M500.00. This figure, however, only acts as a guideline and the number of key posts is negotiable depending upon the merits of each case.

2 For executive posts which require professional qualifications and practical experience, expatriates may be employed up to a maximum period of 10 years. This is subject to the conditions that Malaysians are eventually trained to take over the post.

3 For non-executive posts which require technical skills and experience, expatriates may be employed up to a maximum period of five years subject to the condition that Malaysians are eventually trained to take over the post.

4 Every effort must be made to train more Bumiputras so that the employment pattern at all levels of the organisation will reflect the multi-racial composition of the country.

5 For industries designated by the government as priority industries, such as those which are labour-intensive and heavy manufacturing industries (which are export-oriented), the conditions in i, ii and iii above may be relaxed depending upon the merits of each case.

Application for expatriate posts

Under the new system introduced by the government recently, applications for expatriate posts (including key posts, executive and non-executive posts) can now be submitted to the MIDA at the same time as the company's application for approval of its industrial project. It was previously said that the applications for expatriate posts were submitted separately to the Standing Committee on Malaysianisation through the Immigration Department for its consideration and approval. Letters of approval in principle will thus in future include not only the approval for the project paper, but also the number of expatriate posts approved and their duration.

The above procedure applies for expatriate personnel required by (i) all companies which propose to establish new projects (ii) all existing companies which propose to manufacture additional products (diversification of projects) and (iii) all existing companies which propose to expand their production capacities (expansion of projects).

Addresses of useful contacts

There are several government institutions and agencies of interest to investors, both local and foreign. Listed below are some contacts addresses which may be useful and important to potential investors.

1 Statutory authorities and government agencies

Malaysian Industrial Development Authority (MIDA)
3rd–6th Floor, Wisma Damansara
Jalan Semantan
PO Box 618
Kuala Lumpur
Tel 03–943633

Malaysian Industrial Development Finance Berhad (MIDF)
No. 195A, Jalan Pekeliling
Kuala Lumpur
Tel 03–481166

Malaysian Industrial Estates Sendiri Berhad
No. 195A, Jalan Pekeliling
Kuala Lumpur
Tel 03–483177

Central Bank of Malaysia
Jalan Kucing
PO Box 922
Kuala Lumpur
Tel 03–988044, 989044

Petroleum Nasional (PETRONAS)
Menara Dayabumi
Kuala Lumpur
Tel 03–443833

or

Bangunan Petronas
136, Jalan Pudu
PO Box 2444
Kuala Lumpur
Tel 03–489066

Malaysian Export Credit Insurance Berhad
2nd Floor, Wisma Damansara
Jalan Semantan
Kuala Lumpur
PO Box 1048
Tel 03–949366
Telex MA 31190
Cable EXCRED Kuala Lumpur

National Electricity Board of the States of Malaya
(Lembaga Letrik Negara Tanah Melayu)
129, Jalan Bangsar
PO Box 1003
Kuala Lumpur
Tel 03–445566

Malaysian Rubber Exchange and Licensing Board (MRELB)
(Lembaga Pasaran dan Pelesen Getah Malaysia)
7th Floor, Hong Leong Building
Jalan Bandar
PO Box 531
Kuala Lumpur
Tel 03–87961/4, 03–202594, 03–202611/33

Palm Oil Registration and Licensing Authority (PORLA)
(Lembaga Pendaftaran dan Pelesenan Minyak Kelapa Sawit)
Jalan Dungun
PO Box 2184
Kuala Lumpur
Tel 03–947122
Telex PORLA MA 30097

Malaysian Timber Industry Board
(Lembaga Perindustrian Kayu Malaysia)
5th & 6th Floor, Wisma Bunga Raya
Jalan Ampang
PO Box 887
Kuala Lumpur
Tel 03–486233

The Registrar of Companies
2nd Floor, Block 10
Government Office Complex
Jalan Duta
Kuala Lumpur
Tel 03–947389

Registrar of Societies
(Pendaftar Pertubuhan)
2, Jalan Sentul
PO Box 204
Kuala Lumpur
Tel 03–927577

Registrar of Trade Unions
(Pendaftar Kesatuan Sekerja)
7th Floor, Wisma MPI, Jalan Raja Chulan
Kuala Lumpur
Tel 03–424088

Industrial Court
(Mahkamah Perusahaan)
Jalan Perseketuan
Kuala Lumour 01–01
Tel 03–91221/141/313/414

Employees Provident Fund
(Kumpulan Wang Simpanan Pekerja)
Jalan Gasing
PO Box 202
Petaling Jaya
Selangor
Tel 03–565333

Social Security Organisation (SOCSO)
(Jabatan Pertubuhan Keselamatan Social)
6th Floor, Wisma Keramat, Jalan Gurney
Kuala Lumpur
Tel 03–920310

2 Manufacturers' associations

Federation of Malaysia Manufacturers
8th Floor, Angkasa Raya Building, Jalan Ampang
PO Box 2194
Kuala Lumpur
Tel 03–484011, 03–484174, 03–484271
Telex MA 32437 FMM

C & CA Clement & Concrete Association of Malaysia
8th Floor, Angkasa Raya Building
Jalan Ampang, PO Box 2194
Kuala Lumpur
Tel 03–484251, 03–484011

Malaysia Ceramic Industry Group
8th Floor, Angkasa Raya Building
Jalan Ampang, PO Box 2194
Kuala Lumpur
Tel 03–484251, 03–484011

Chemical Industries Council of Malaysia (CICM)
8th Floor, Angkasa Raya Building
Jalan Ampang
Kuala Lumpur
Tel 03–484251, 03–484011

Malaysian Food Processing Industry Group
8th Floor, Angkasa Raya Building
Jalan Ampang
PO Box 2194
Kuala Lumpur
Tel 03–484251, 03–484011

Malaysia Electrical, Electronic & Allied
Industries Group (MEAG)
8th Floor, Angkasa Raya Building
Jalan Ampang
Kuala Lumpur
Tel 03–474251, 03–484011

Malaysian Iron & Steel Industry Federation (MISIF)
8th Floor, Angkasa Raya Building
Jalan Ampang
PO Box 2194
Kuala Lumpur
Tel 03–484251, 03–484011

Malaysian Rubber Products Manufacturers Association
c/o MRRDB, Bangunan Getah Asli
PO Box 508
Kuala Lumpur
Tel 03–484422, 03–484513, 03–484690
Telex MRRDB 30953

Palm Oil Refiners Association of Malaysia (PORIM)
1006, 10th Floor, Wisma MPI, Jalan Raja Chulan
Kuala Lumpur
Tel 03–498916, 03–488993
Telex MA 31337

Malaysia Textile Manufacturers Association
Suite T019, 3rd Floor, Sungei Wang Plaza
Jalan Bukit Bintang
Kuala Lumpur
Tel 03–486454, 486587

Malaysian Plastics Manufacturers Association
37, Jalan 20/4
Petaling Jaya
Selangor
Tel 03–763027

The Furniture Manufacturers & Traders Federation
of Malaysia
75–1, Jalan Mega Mandung, Bandar Kompleks
Batu 5, Jalan Kelang Lama
Kuala Lumpur
Tel 03–725708, 03–725877

Malaysian Plywood Manufacturers Association
36A, Jalan Telawi
Kuala Lumpur
Tel 03–948062, 03–943357

Malaysian Pharmaceutical Trade & Manufacturers Association
31A, Jalan SS 21/37
Damansara Utama
Petaling Jaya
Selangor
Tel 03–785754

Malaysian Footwear Manufacturers Association
21–4, Jalan Barat
Kuala Lumpur
Tel 03–412174

3 Trade centres and primary producers' associations

Malaysian Export Trade Centre
Wisma PKNS
Jalan Raja Laut
Kuala Lumpur
Tel 03–928122

The Kuala Lumpur Commodity Exchange
Wisma Stephens
Jalan Raja Chulan
Kuala Lumpur
Tel 03–413411

The Kuala Lumpur Stock Exchange
Kompleks Pejabat Damansara
Jalan Duta
Kuala Lumpur
Tel 03–947167, 03–946433

Malaysian Rubber Producers' Council
Jalan Ampang
Kuala Lumpur
Tel 03–482677, 03–482713

Malaysian Oil Palm Growers' Council
Wisma Bunga Raya
Jalan Ampang
Kuala Lumpur
Tel 03–425088, 03–425471

States of Malaya Chamber of Mines
Bangunan Ming
Jalan Bukit Nenas
Kuala Lumpur
Tel 03–228461, 03–228462

4 Chambers of commerce

Malaysian International Chamber of Commerce & Industry
8th Floor, Wisma Damansara, Jalan Semantan
PO Box 192, Kuala Lumpur
Tel 03–942117, 03–941690
Cable Address Commerce Kuala Lumpur
Telex COMER MA 32120

National Chamber of Commerce & Industry of Malaysia,
Angkasa Raya Building
Jalan Ampang
Kuala Lumpur
Tel 03–435004
Cable Address NICIM
Telex MA 37604

Malay Chamber of Commerce and Industry of Malaysia,
13th Floor, Angkasa Raya Building
Jalan Ampang
Kuala Lumpur
Tel 03–433090

Associated Chinese Chambers of Commerce and Industry of Malaysia,
Ground Floor, Chinese Assembly Hall
1, Jalan Maharajalela (Jalan Birch)
Kuala Lumpur 08–02
Tel 03–220473, 03–280278
Cable Address ASOCHINMA KUALA LUMPUR

Associated Indian Chambers of Commerce Malaysia,
18, Jalan Tun Perak
PO Box 675
Kuala Lumpur
Tel 03–920255, 03–920351, 03–920459
Telex & Answerback MA 320477 UBAID
Cable Address STEELHOUSE

5 Research and development organisations

Standard and Industrial Research Institute of Malaysia (SIRIM)
(Institut Piawaian dan Penyelidikan Perindustrian Malaysia)
Lot 10810, Phase III, Federal Highway
PO Box 35
Shah Alam
Selangor
Tel 03–36201/2/3/4

Malaysian Agricultural Research and Development Institute (MARDI)
(Institut Penyelidikan dan Kemajuan Pertanian Malaysia)
PO Box 2301
GPO Kuala Lumpur 01–02
Tel 03–356601 (12 lines) (Serdang)

Rubber Research Institute of Malaysia
(Institut Penyelidikan Getah Malaysia)
260, Jalan Ampang
PO Box 150
Kuala Lumpur
Tel 03–467033

Malaysian Rubber Research and Development Board (MRRDB)
(Lembaga Penyelidikan dan Kemajuan Getah Malaysia)
Bangunan Getah Asli, 150 Jalan Ampang
PO Box 508
Kuala Lumpur
Tel 03–484422, 03–484513

The Tin Industry (Research & Development) Board
6th Floor, Ming Building
Jalan Bukit Nenas
PO Box 2560
Kuala Lumpur
Tel 03–228461, 03–228462

Palm Oil Research Institute of Malaysia (PORIM)
Wisma Central
PO Box 620
Kuala Lumpur
Tel 03–431303, 485277
Telex MA 31544

National Productivity Centre
(Pusat Daya Pengeluaran Negara)
PO Box 64
Petaling Jaya
Selangor
Tel 03–563688, 03–563731, 03–563812, 03–563905, 03–563602

Appendixes

1 Postal and telephone rates effective 1 Jan. 1983

Types	Weights	New rate (from 1 Jan. 1983)
		$ c
Letters	up to 20g	0.20
	20 to 50g	0.30
	50 to 100g	0.45
	100 to 250g	0.85
	250 to 500g	1.50
	500 to 1 000g	2.50
	1 000to 2 000g	4.00
Postcard		0.15
Small parcels	up to 100g	0.20
	100 to 250g	0.35
	250 to 500g	0.50
	500 to 1 000g	0.95
Printed matter	up to 50g	0.15
	50 to 100g	0.20
	100 to 250g	0.25
	250 to 500g	0.40
	500 to 1 000g	0.65
	1 000 to 2 000g	1.00
	every extra 1 000g	0.50
Newspapers (provided in Malaysia or Singapore)	up to 100g	0.15
	100 to 250g	0.20
	250 to 500g	0.35
	500 to 1 000g	0.50
	1 000 to 2 000g	0.80

Telephone rental

Area	*Business customers* $	*Domestic customers* $
Town		
Exchange capacity		
Exceeding 10 000 (multi-exchange)	420	240
Small towns		
10 000–500	360	204
Rural		
Less than 500	240	120
Urban	SABAH	
Exceeding 500 (multi-exchange)	300	204
Rural		
Less than 500	240	120
Urban	SARAWAK	
Exceeding 500 (multi-exchange)	300	204
Rural		
Less than 500	240	120

Distance	Full rate	Reduced rates
Local calls	10 cents per unit	"
Long distance calls	$	$
Not exceeding 50km	0.30	0.20
50 km to 150 km	0.90	0.50
150 km to 550 km	2.40	1.20
Over 550 km	4.50	3.00

2 List of priority products

A list of 'priority products' has been approved by the Minister of Trade and Industry and the Minister of Finance. The list includes:

Manufacture of wooden, metal, plastic, rubber and textile toys

Manufacture from padi husks and straw

(a) Gazetted in 1970

Manufacture of food products

Fruit canning excluding pineapple canning, vegetable canning

Meat canning including meat, poultry, game and preparations thereof but excluding chicken and mutton curries

Manufacture of animal feedstuffs

Pineapple waste and bran

Manufacture of wood products

Fibreboard, chipboard, softboard, hardboard

Manufacture of rubber products

Rubberised fabrics, conveyor belts, transmission belts, V-type belts
Rubber insulated and braided cables

Manufacture of chemicals and chemical products

Titanium dioxide

Manufacture of hardware tools

Axes, pliers
Screw drivers
Spanners
Riveting tools
Hammers, pincers

Manufacture of industrial machinery and parts

Ball bearings
Machine tools
Industrial machinery all types

(b) Gazetted in 1972

Manufacture of refrigerating, exhaust, ventilating and air-conditioning machinery

Room air-conditioners
Compressors and parts and components of air-conditioners, 90 per cent of which is for export

(c) Gazetted in 1973

Primary iron and steel-milling (by integrated process)

Cast pig iron
Steel ingots or billets
Mild steel round bars
Mild steel angle bars
Mild steel flat bars
High tensile deformed bars
Wire rods

(d) Gazetted in 1975

Manufacture of wood products

Knock-down furniture
Wooden souvenir and handicraft items
Wooden sports equipment
Wooden educational objects
Turned wood objects
Rayon
Pulp and paper

Manufacture of natural rubber products

Swimming accessories of rubber (90% for export)
Sporting goods or rubber
Dipped rubber products (90 per cent for export)
Inflatable rubber products (90 per cent for export)
Tyres—all types (90 per cent for export)

Rubber shoes and boots (90 per cent for export)
Rubber masterbatch (90 per cent for export)
Tubing/hoses (90 per cent for export)
Cot sheets (90 per cent for export)
Rubber mats and other moulded rubber products (90 per cent for export)
Rubber floor tiles (90 per cent for export)
Medical and surgical rubber products (90 per cent for export)

Manufacture of chemicals and chemical products

Upgrading of ilmenite and rutile
Palm oil derivatives in finished products

Manufacture of agricultural implements

Cangkul
Spade
Rake
Tajak
Sickle
Tuai
Tapping knives

Primary iron and steel-milling (by integrated process)

Sponge iron
Steel blooms and slabs
Hot rolled structural sections such as I-steel, channel steel, I-steel and H-steel
Steel plates
Hot rolled coils
Cold rolled coils

Steel castings and ferro alloys

Alloyed steel castings
Ferro-silicon
Ferro-manganese
Ferro-silico-manganese
Ferro-chromium

Manufacture of electronic and electrical components and products (90 per cent for export)

Television sets
electronic computers
Weather communication equipment
Hearing aids
Walkie-Talkie sets
Radiograms/stereograms
gramaphones/record players/record changers
Fish finders
Testing meters and instruments
Telephone and telegraph line system
Telecommuniciation equipment including radio and TV broadcasting equipment

X-ray apparatus
Integrated circuits
Television picture tubes
Valves
Volume/tone controls
Potentiometers
Tuners for TV sets
Antenna and oscillating coils
Peaking coils
Magnetic head coils/recording heads
Input, output, vertical and horizontal transformers, and chokers for radios, TV sets and amplifiers
Memory planes/units
Earphone
Modules
Magnetic audio tape cassette reels
Parts for hearing aids
Speakers
Microphones
Circuit packers
Telephone amplifiers
Matrix planes
Memory core arrays and its components
Digital heads
Magnetic advice for digital and other computer memory systems
Plastic moulded cabinets
Plastic knobs
Radio chassis
Coil formers
TV aerials
Radiogram/stereogram chasis
Electronic heaters
Computing scales
Timers
Digital clocks
Transducers
Miniature (micro) motors
Counters
Card readers
Automatic gate systems
A-D, D-A converters
Scanners
Annunciators
Shift registers
Sequence programmers
Automatic fare collection systems
Automatic traffic control system
Automatic vending systems
Automatic parking fee collection systems
Automatic cytological analysers

The following products of integrated manufacture:

fans
vacuum cleaners
cooking and kitchen wares
shavers
hair dryers
fractional horsepower motors

Leather cases and plastic and metal parts for transistor radios

Tools and dies for electronic industries
Hi-fi stereo and cassette players

Manufacture of machinery (90 per cent for export)

Refrigerators
Air-conditioners (package unit and automobile)
Typewriters
Calculators
Dictaphones
Cash registers
Accounting machines
Machine tools and mechanical precision measuring equipment
Power-driven hand tools

Manufacture of professional, scientific, measuring and controlling equipment (90 per cent for export)

Surgical and dental instruments and equipments
Hearing aids
Scientific gauges of all types

Manufacture of photographic and optical goods (90 per cent for export)

Cameras—all types
Projectors—all types
Lenses
Binoculars
Telescope magnifying glass and microscopes

Manufacture of watches and clocks (90 per cent for export)

Watches—all types
Clocks—all types

Manufacture of musical instruments (90 per cent export)

Musical instruments—all types

(e) Gazetted in 1979

Manufacture of electronic and electrical components and products (90 per cent for export)

TV deflection yoke
Flyback transformer
Electric automatic pencil sharpener
Vacuum cleaner for motor-cars
Electric home water pumps

3 Summary of industrial investment procedure in Malaysia

Item	Description
Investment procedure	(1) The Malaysian Industrial Development Authority (MIDA)—pre-investment studies, handling inquiries from potential investors, evaluating applications from companies seeking special status and provision of technical advisory services (2) Investors need initially deal with only one agency to obtain (i) an initial step or (ii) subsequent approval of an application to establish a manufacturing facility
Investment incentive	(1) Tax relief for pioneer status investment, enterprise which is located in a development area, priority product items and percentage of Malaysian content is > 50 per cent (2) Investment tax credit for approved companies not having pioneer status, which will be not less than 25 per cent of the total capital expenditure involved (3) 40 per cent capital allowance for expanding is exempted if the project is in national interest
Infrastructure support	(1) Electricity supplies: by a network of 18 thermal and hydro-power stations and diesel stations (2) Water supplies
Restriction of foreign ownership	(1) Prefer joint-venture basis between Malaysian and foreigner (2) Project depends to a very large extent on the Malaysian market and depletes Malaysian resources, requires a substantial Malaysian majority (3) Export-oriented project can be given to foreign majority ownership depending on the size of project, location, nature of product manufactured, level of technology and number of similar projects already established
Exchange regulation	(1) Malaysian government practices liberal exchange control regulations (2) Foreign investors can bring in required capital for approved projects and are able to remit capital and profits with minimal government control (3) Under Article VII of International Monetary Fund's Articles of Association assumes a free transfer of funds for international transactions

Item	Description
Labour supply	(1) Labour force: 4.5 m. (2) Labour rates and productivity tend to favour industries which are labour intensive and export-oriented
Wage level	(1) Wage for unskilled workers—$M8 per day (2) Semi-unskilled workers—$M10–12 per day (3) Skilled workers—$M15.20 per day (4) Secretary—$M350 per month

4 Information on industrial estates in Malaysia as at 30 June 1982

Industrial estate	Location state	TOTAL Total area still available (hectares)	Selling price per sq.m. ($M)	Quit rent ($M) per hectare, per annum	Lease period years
Bayan Lepas	Penang	30.80	31.22–53.82	2 149.81	60
Bayan Lepas FTZ—Phase I	Penang	0	53.82	2 149.81	60
Phase I	Penang	0.98	53.82	2 149.81	60
Phase III	Penang	25.94.94	32.29	2 149.81	60
Prai	Penang	327.96	24.22–33.91	1 717.38	60
Prai FTZ	Penang	68.27	26.91–29.60	2 149.81	60
Prai Wharf FTZ	Penang	4.82	NA	NA	NA
Mak Mandin	Penang	7.16	NA	NA	60
Seberang Jaya	Penang	32.58	NA	NA	NA
Pulau Jerejak	Penang	107.00	NA	NA	NA
Tasek	Perak	0	3.77– 5.38	294.53	99
Jelapang	Perak	0	5.81– 6.46	2 322.79	60
Kamunting	Perak	0	8.61–10.76	74.13	99
Parit Buntar	Perak	0	10.76	741.31	60
Kuala Kangsar	Perak	0	10.76	968.90	60
Tupai I & II	Perak	0	5.38– 8.91	2 594.60	60
Shah Alam	Selangor	0	26.90–32.29	10.76 per sq.m.	99
Petaling Jaya (Section 51A)	Selangor	0	24.95–26.90	3% of premium	99
Petaling Jaya (Selatan)	Selangor	44.18	21.52–59.20	16.14 per sq.m.	99
Other Areas	Selangor	0	24.95–26.90	3% of premium	99
Pandamaran	Selangor	8.40	17.76–21.50	3% of premium	99
Telok Panglima Garang	Selangor	13.05	43.05	9.68 per sq.m.	99
Telok Panglima Garang FTZ	Selangor	2.44	18.83–43.05	9.68 per sq.m.	99

Industrial estate	Location state	TOTAL Total area still available (hectares)	Selling price per sq.m. ($M)	Quit rent ($M) per hectare, per annum	Lease period years
Batu Caves	Selangor	1.24	16.14–53.81	3% of premium	99
Sungai Way/Subang (FTZ)	Selangor	2.42	16.14–53.81	3% of premium	99
Ampang/Ulu Klang (FTZ)	Selangor	0	16.14	3% of premium	99
Ampang/Ulu Klang	Selangor	0	32.29	3% of premium	99
Selat Klang Utara	Selangor	49.86	86.11	32.29 per sq.m.	99
Bangi	Selangor	129.82	26.90–80.72	19.37 per sq.m.	99
Bukit Rajah	Selangor	33.24	107.63	19.37 per sq.m.	99
Inch Kenneth (Kajang)	Selangor	13.41	43.05	3% of premium	99
Setapak	Federal Territory	34.65	32.29	3% of premium	99
Jejawi	Perlis	10.12	26.91–30.14	NA	NA
Gong Badak	Trengganu	25.57	17.28	543.40	60
Kuala Ibai	Trengganu	2 191.37	27.00	543.40	60
Jakar I & II	Trengganu	10.42	27.00	543.40	60
Dungun	Trengganu	7.49	30.24	543.40	60
Bukit Besi	Trengganu	70.1	(proposed) 2.23– 8.36 per sq.m.	(proposed) 4.00 per 185 sq.m. or at least 5.00 per lot	60
Durian Mas	Trengganu	50.32	2.23– 8.36 per sq.m.	NA	60
Rasau Kerteh	Trengganu	24.15	2.23– 8.36 per sq.m.	NA	60

Industrial estate	Location state	TOTAL Total area still available (hectares)	Selling price per sq.m. ($M)	Quit rent ($M) per hectare, per annum	Lease period years
Ulu Cukai	Trengganu	29.08	2.23– 8.36 per sq.m.	4.40 per 92.90 sq.m. or at least 10.00 per lot	60
Cenih	Trengganu	70.77	2.23– 8.36 per sq.m.	NA	60
Pengkalan Chepa I	Kelantan	0	6.46–21.53	7.00	66
Pengkalan Chepa II	Kelantan	86.20	16.15	7.00	66
Tanah Merah	Kelantan	0	44 478–74 131 per hectare	7.00	66
Jeli	Kelantan	0	9 928.68 per hectare	7.00	66
Gua Musang	Kelantan	40.47	NA	7.00	66
Lundang	Kelantan	0	Ready-built factory buildings	NA	33 years with option for another 3 years
Senawang	Negeri Sembilan	0	5.38	1 976.84	99
Dioh	Negeri Sembilan	0	7.53	1 976.84	60
Chembong	Negeri Sembilan	3.64	12.92–20.45	1 976.84	60
Sg. Gadut	Negeri Sembilan	2.27	5.38–12.49	1 976.84	60
Simpang Pertang	Negeri Sembilan	3.82	NA	NA	NA

Industrial estate	Location state	TOTAL Total area still available (hectares)	Selling price per sq.m. ($M)	Quit rent ($M) per hectare, per annum	Lease period years
Larkin and Tampoi	Johor	0	4.31	484.33	60 years and 3 years option
Pasir Gudang	Johor	95.10	32.29–43.06	494.21 for light industries 741.32 for medium industries 988.42 for heavy industries	
Tanjung Agas	Johor	2.02	21.53–32.29		
Tongkang Pecah	Johor	0	12.92–16.15		
Senai	Johor	1.62	21.53–32.29		
Segamat	Johor	0	21.53–32.29		
Parit Raja	Johor	8.09	21.53–32.29		
Sri Gading	Johor	0	32.29–37.67		
Kota Tinggi	Johor	5.66	37.67–43.06		
Kluang	Johor	NA	NA		
Likas (Phase I)	Sabah	0	7.53	3% of premium	60
Likas (Phase II)	Sabah	0	29.06		60
Sandakan	Sabah	0	290.63 including building		60
Lok Kawi Estate	Sabah	0	64.50		
Tawau	Sabah	8.78	NA	NA	60
Tandat	Sabah	0	NA	NA	60
Pending	Sarawak	11.81	12.38–13.99	840.16	60
Upper Lanang	Sarawak	3.24	25.83	741.32	60
Piasau (Phase I)	Sarawak	0	5.30	617.75	60

Industrial estate	Location state	TOTAL Total area still available (hectares)	Selling price per sq.m. ($M)	Quit rent ($M) per hectare, per annum	Lease period years
Bintulu Service Industrial Estate	Sarawak	0.39	91.49	NA	60
Kiduroy Service Industrial Estate	Sarawak	8.17	NA	NA	60
Ayer Keroh	Malacca	0	21.53	3% of land value	99
Batu Berendam FTZ	Malacca	5.75	26.91	434.90	99
Tanjong Kling FTZ	Malacca	0	9.15	434.90	99
Tanjong Kling (Phase II)	Malacca	32.25	21.53	322.92/1 000 sq.m.	99
Alor Gajah	Malacca	1.17	16.15	322.92/1 000 sq.m.	99
Bukit Rambai	Malacca	3.72	19.38	333.68/1 000 sq.m.	99
Merlimau	Malacca	13.49	12.92	322.92/1 000 sq.m.	99
Bakar Arang	Kedah	14.65	8.60–10.80	88.15	60 years and option for extension of 39 years

Industrial estate	Location state	TOTAL Total area still available (hectares)	Selling price per sq.m. ($M)	Quit rent ($M) per hectare, per annum	Lease period years
Kulim	Kedah	57.1	8.60–10.80	88.15	
Tikam Batu	Kedah	0	6.50–7.50	88.15	60 years
Mergong II	Kedah	0	5.40–16.20	88.15	and option
Mergong II (Extension)	Kedah	0	NA	88.15	for extension
Mergong Barrage	Kedah	0	10.80–26.90	88.15	of 39 years
Kuala Kedah	Kedah	4.2	4.30 (unfilled land)	88.15	
Semambu	Pahang	17.65	37.67	543.63	66
Peramu	Pahang	16.68.68	9.69	543.63	66
Songsang	Pahang	9.50	14.00	543.63	66
Maran	Pahang	3.62	15.07	543.63	66
Jerantut	Pahang	1.84	18.30	2,174.52	66
Gebeng	Pahang	149.30	26.91	543.63	66
Bentong	Pahang	41.31	37.67	543.63	66
Mu'adzam Shah	Pahang	8.30	7.75	53.82/1 000 sq.m. or $40 per lot	60 years with option for another 30 years

NA Data not available

Proposed industrial estates not shown on industrial estate map

Proposed industrial estate	Location state	Planned aea (hectares)
Tanjong Kling Expansion	Malacca	—
Bukit Rambai Expansion	Malacca	105.22
Nilai	Negeri Sembilan	121.41
Tampin	Negeri Sembilan	12.14
Seremban (Jalan Pantai)	Negeri Sembilan	15.38
Beranang (Ulu Langat District)	Selangor	141.64
Banting Phase I	Selangor	19.02
Banting Phase II	Selangor	27.92
Sungai Besar	Selangor	5.66
Kuala Selangor	Selangor	77.70
Pandamaran Jaya	Selangor	26.70
Kalumpang, Ulu Selangor	Selangor	14.29
Sekinchan	Selangor	28.32
Sungai Choh	Selangor	8.09
Taman Meru	Perak	48.22
Kampong Acheh	Perak	586.76
Tupai Phase III	Perak	16.39
Jalan Silibin	Perak	80.13
Menglembu	Perak	116.55
Grik I	Perak	8.09
Seri Manjong—Sitiawan	Perak	32.37
Tanjung Pauh	Kedah	80.90
Rompin	Pahang	103.60
Telok Kelong	Trengganu	1 214.57
Kerteh Industrial Estate	Trengganu	485.62
Kemubu	Kelantan	60.70
Jeli	Kelantan	142.04
Piasau (Phase II)	Sarawak	60.70
Petra Jaya	Sarawak	270.33
Limbang	Sarawak	9.71
Betong, Sarikei and Bandar Sri Aman	Sarawak	12.34
Crossing Industrial Estate	Sarawak	146.50
Lahad Datu	Sabah	1.62

Source: Malaysian Industrial Development Authority

5 Schedule of registration fees for domestic companies

	$M
For registration of a company whose authorised capital does not exceed $M25 000	300
For registration of a company whose authorised capital exceeds $M25 000, the above fee of $M300 plus the following additional fees regulated according to the amount of authorised capital:	
• For every $M5 000 of authorised capital or part of $M5 000 after the first $M25 000 up to $M500 000	20
• For every $M5 000 of authorised capital or part of $M5 000 after the first $M500 000 up to $M1 000 000	10
• For every $M15 000 of authorised capital or part of $M15 000 after the first $M1 000 000 up to $M50 000 000	5
• For every $M20 000 of authorised capital or part of $M20 000 after the first $M50 000 000	3

Translating the foregoing rules into schedule, the registration fees applicable on a specific amount of authorised capital are:

Authorised capital $M	*Registration fee* $M
25 000	300
30 000	320
35 000	340
40 000	360
45 000	380
50 000	400
60 000	440
70 000	480
80 000	520
90 000	560
100 000	600
150 000	800
200 000	1 000
250 000	1 200
300 000	1 400
350 000	1 600
400 000	1 800
450 000	2 000
500 000	2 200
600 000	2 400
700 000	2 600
800 000	2 800
900 000	3 000
1 000 000	3 200
1 500 000	3 370
2 000 000	3 535

Authorised capital $M	*Registration fee* $M
2 500 000	3 700
3 000 000	3 800
4 000 000	4 200
5 000 000	4 535
10 000 000	6 200
15 000 000	7 870
20 000 000	9 535
25 000 000	11 200
30 000 000	12 870
35 000 000	14 535
40 000 000	16 200
45 000 000	17 870
50 000 000	19 535
60 000 000	21 035
70 000 000	22 535
80 000 000	24 035
90 000 000	25 535
100 000 000	27 035
110 000 000	28 535
120 000 000	30 035
130 000 000	31 535
140 000 000	33 035
150 000 000	34 535
Over $M150 000 000	Incremental fee of $M3 for every $M20 000 additional authorised capital but only up to a maximum registration fee of $M35 000

The fee for registering a foreign branch operation in Malaysia is one-half of the fee for incorporating a local company with the same amount of authorised capital.

To illustrate:

Authorised capital $M	*Registration fee* $M
500 000	1 100
1 000 000	1 600
10 000 000	3 100

Endnotes

Chapter 1

1 Malaysia *Economic Report, 1984/85* Malaysia: Ministry of Finance Malaysia, 1984
2 There is some controversy regarding the exact date of the founding of Malacca and the historical record of early Malacca. For more details regarding this, see Wang Gung Wu *Community and Nation: Essays on Southeast Asia and The Chinese* Kuala Lumpur: Heinemann, 1981, Sir Richard Winstedt *Malaya and Its History* London: Hutchinson, 1966, and K. G. Tregouning *A History of Modern Malaya* London: Eastern Universities Press, 1964
3 This version of early Malacca history is based on Sir Richard Winstedt's *Malaya and Its History* London: Hutchinson, 1966
4 There are a number of references for the materials in this section. These include G. P. Means *Malaysian Politics* London: Hodder and Stoughton, 1976, J. M. Gullick *Malaya* London: Ernest Benn, 1964 and D. R. Snodgrass *Inequality and Economic Development in Malaysia* Kuala Lumpur: Oxford University Press, 1980
5 The material for this section is based on a number of references. These include K. Young, W. C. F. Bussink and P. Hassan (eds) *Malaysia: Growth and Equity in a Multiracial Society* Baltimore: Johns Hopkins University Press, 1980, Tan Sri Mohd Suffian Hashim *An Introduction to the Constitution of Malaysia* Kuala Lumpur: Government Printer, 1972, and Malaysia *Informaion Malaysia* Kuala Lumpur: Berita Publishing Sdn Bhd, various years
6 Malaysia *Second Malaysia Plan 1971–75* Kuala Lumpur: Government Printer, 1971, 1
7 Malaysia *Mid-Term Review, Second Malaysia Plan 1971–75* Kuala Lumpur: Government Printer, 1973
8 There are numerous references which discuss NEP. These include E.K. Fisk, and H. Osman-Rani *The Political Economy of Malaysia* Kuala Lumpur: Oxford University Press, 1982, D. R. Snodgrass *Inequality and Economic Development in Malaysia* Kuala Lumpur: Oxford University Press, 1980, S. Anand *Inequality and Poverty in Malaysia: Measurement and Decomposition* New York: Oxford University Press, 1983

Chapter 2

1 World Bank *World Development Report, 1984* New York: Oxford University Press, 1984
2 Malaysia *Fourth Malaysia Plan, 1981–85* Kuala Lumpur: Government Printer, 1981
3 Refer to the Malays and other indigenous groups of the country.
4 See, for example, Tan Koon Swan 'Public Enterprise: Restructuring and Chinese Capital Under the New Economic Policy' Paper presented at the Seventh Malaysian Economic Convention, Kuala Lumpur, 1983. An example of the vastness of government resources are the proposed petrochemical and steel projects in Trengganu, Sarawak, and Sabah. In total, they called for an investment of $M10.07 billion. Assuming 30 per cent equity, this would amount to a total of $M3.02 billion. As a comparison, for 1981 the 613 industrial projects approved have a proposed called-up investment of $M1.71 billion, a substantial proportion of which is also Bumiputra equity
5 World Bank *World Development Report 1980* New York: Oxford University Press, 1980
6 Between the period 1974–81, Malaysia's exports to East Asia (excluding Japan) have increased from 30.4 per cent (of its total export) to 38.2 per cent. Similarly, over the corresponding period, Malaysia's exports to the West (including Japan) have declined from 57.6 per cent to 51.4 per cent

Chapter 3

1 B. J. L. Berry, 'An Inductive Approach to the Regionalisation of Economic Development' in N. Ginsburg, (ed.) *Essays on Geography and Economic Development* Chicago: University of Chicago Press, 1960
2 Malaysia *Third Malaysia Plan, 1976–80* Kuala Lumpur: Government Printer, 1976
3 This chapter is based on materials presented in the various Malaysian Plans, particularly the Fourth Malaysian Plan (Malaysia *Fourth Malaysia Plan 1981–85* Kuala Lumpur: Government Printer, 1981 and Malaysia *Mid-Term Review of the Fourth Malaysia Plan 1981–85* Kuala Lumpur: Government Printer, 1984) and Kadir H. Din 'The Physical Infrastructure' chapter 3 in E. K. Fisk, and H. Osman-Rani (eds) *The Political Economy of Malaysia* Kuala Lumpur: Oxford University Press, 1982, 44–65. Some of the materials quoted are collected from interviews with the relevant government agencies

Chapter 4

1 Malaysia *Money and Banking in Malaysia* Bank Negara: Economic Research and Statistics Department, 1979, 279
2 Eugene F. Fama 'Tomorrow at the NYSE' *Journal of Business* vol. 38, 1965, 34–105
3 L. Nasir 'A Study of Market Efficiency and Risk Return Relationship in the Malaysian Capital Market' Doctoral Dissertation, Katholieke Universiteit Leuven, 1983, 26–38

Chapter 5

1 Malaysia *General Report of the Housing Census* Population and Housing Census of Malaysia 1980, Kuala Lumpur: Department of Statistics, 1983, 25
2 Malaysia *Labour and Manpower Report 1980* Kuala Lumpur: Ministry of Labour, 1981, 71
3 Malaysia *Labour and Manpower Report 1981/82* Kuala Lumpur: Ministry of Labour, 1984, 67
4 Ibid
5 Ibid 49

Chapter 6

1 Malaysia *Fourth Malaysia Plan 1981–85* Kuala Lumpur: Government Printer, 1981
2 For a classical account of this, see James Puthucheary *Ownership and control of the Malaysian Economy* Singapore: Eastern Universities Press Ltd, 1960
3 Malaysia *Census of Distributive Trades* Kuala Lumpur: Department of Statistics, 1981

Chapter 8

1 Bank Negara Malaysia *Annual Report 1983* Kuala Lumpur: Bank Negara, 1983
2 Ho Ngan Kuang and Cheong Koon Tian 'Pre-Feasibility Study on: Oil Palm Cultivation and Pepper Cultivation' Faculty of Economics and Administration, Kuala Lumpur: University of Malaya, 1984, 3
3 Ibid 22
4 Lai Nyok Kem and Cheong Koon Tian 'Pre-Feasibility Study of Cocoa and Rubber Cultivation' Faculty of Economics and Administration, Kuala Lumpur: University of Malaya, 1984, 26
5 Ho Ngan Kuang and Cheong Koon Tian 'Pre-Feasibility Study on: Oil Palm Cultivation and Pepper Cultivation' 25
6 Bank Negara Malaysia *Annual Report 1983* Kuala Lumpur: Bank Negara 1983
7 'Palm Oil Production To Be Increased' *New Straits Times* 30 November 1984
8 Lai Nyok Kim and Foong Soon Yau, 'Pre-Feasibility Study of Cocoa and Rubber Cultivation' 56
9 Chia Song Kun and Mok Suan Sai 'Pre-Feasibility Study on Fishery-Offshore, Inland and Marine Services' Faculty of Economics and Administration, Kuala Lumpur: University of Malaya, 1984, 52
10 Ibid
11 Lee Ching and Lo Ling 'Pre-Feasibility Study on Mining and Exploration in Oil and Gas' Faculty of Economics and Administration, Kuala Lumpur: University of Malaya, 1984, 27
12 Ibid 7
13 Ishak Pateh Akhir 'The Current Status of the Malaysian Tyre Industry' Paper presented to Seminar on Malaysia as a potential major exporter of tyres, Institute of Strategic and International Studies, Kuala Lumpur, September 1984, 6

14 Hidde Smit, *The World Rubber Economy to the Year 2000* Amsterdam: North-Holland, 1982
15 Lembaga Kemajuan Pahang Tenggara 'Secondary Processing of Palm Oil' Study of Industrial Potential in Pahang Tenggara. Feasibility Study No. 1, Kuantan: Lembaga Kemajuan Pahang Tenggara, 1976
16 Malaysia *Forest Statistics, Peninsular Malaysia, 1971–78* Kuala Lumpur: Department of Forestry, 1979
17 Tan See Yin and Rosalind Wong Yuk Mei 'Pre-Feasibility Study for Tourist and Hotel Development' Faculty of Economics and Administration, Kuala Lumpur: University of Malaya, 1984, 86
18 Chua Chin Pen and Ng Hong Huai 'Pre-Feasibility Study on New Investment Opportunities on Fast Food, Franchising and Retailing' Faculty of Economics and Administration, Kuala Lumpur: University of Malaya, 1984; 2

References

Anand S. *Inequality and Poverty in Malaysia: Measurement and Decomposition* New York: Oxford University Press, 1983

Berry B. J. L. 'An Inductive Approach to the Regionalisation of Economic Development' in Ginsburg, N. (ed) *Essays on Geography and Economic Development* Chicago: University of Chicago Press, 1960

Choudhry N.S. *Socio-Economic Sample Survey of Households—Malaysia, 1967–68: Employment and Unemployment* Kuala Lumpur: Department of Statistics, 1970

Fama F. Eugene 'Tomorrow at the NYSE' *Journal of Business* vol. 38, 1965

Fisk E.K. and H. Osman-Rani *The Political Economy of Malaysia* Kuala Lumpur: Oxford University Press, 1982

Fong Chan Onn 'Doing Business in Malaysia' Working Paper, Faculty of Economics and Administration, Kuala Lumpur: University of Malaya, June 1982

—— 'Structure and Opportunities in Malaysian Business' Faculty of Economics and Administration, University of Malaya, Kuala Lumpur, Paper presented to the Academy of International Business International Meeting, June 1984, Singapore

—— *Technological Leap: Malaysian Industry in Transition* Kuala Lumpur: Oxford University Press, 1984

Gullick J.M. *Malaya* London: Ernest Benn, 1964

Kadir H. Din 'The Physical Infrastructure' Chapter 3 in Fisk E.K. and H. Osman-Rani (eds) *The Political Economy of Malaysia* Kuala Lumpur: Oxford University Press, 1982

KLSE Gazette Jan. 1974 and Jun. 1983

Kuala Lumpur Stock Exchange, primary records kept by KLSE, Kuala Lumpur

Malaysia *Annual Statistics of External Trade* vol. 1, 1970, 1975 and 1978, Department of Statistics, Kuala Lumpur

——— *Bank Negara Annual Reports* Bank Negara Malaysia, Kuala Lumpur, various years

——— *Bank Negara Annual Report 1983* Bank Negara Malaysia, Kuala Lumpur, 1984

——— *Bank Negara Report 1971–83* Bank Negara Malaysia, Kuala Lumpur

——— *Bank Negara Quarterly Economic Bulletin, December 1981* Bank Negara Malaysia, Kuala Lumpur, 1981

——— *Bank Negara Quarterly Economic Bulletin, December 1983* Bank Negara Malaysia, 1983

——— *Census of Distributive Trades* Department of Statistics, Kuala Lumpur, 1981

——— *Census of Distributive Trades* Department of Statistics, Kuala Lumpur, various years

——— *Census of Manufacturing Industries/Industrial Surveys* Department of Statistics, Kuala Lumpur, various years

——— *Corporate Planning Department, Petronas, Kuala Lumpur, 1982*

——— *Economic Report 1984/85* Ministry of Finance, Malaysia, 1984

——— *Economic Report*, Ministry of Finance, Kuala Lumpur, various years

——— *Fourth Malaysia Plan 1981–85* Kuala Lumpur: Government Printer, 1981

——— *General Report of the Housing Census* Population and Housing Census of Malaysia, 1980, Department of Statistics, Kuala Lumpur 1983

——— *Information Malaysia* Berita Publishing Sdn Bhd Kuala Lumpur, various years

——— *Investment Incentives Act 1983 (Revised—1978)* Malaysian Industrial Development Authority, Kuala Lumpur, 1980

——— *Labour and Manpower Report 1980* Ministry of Labour, Kuala Lumpur, 1981

——— *Labour and Manpower Report 1981/82* Ministry of Labour, Kuala Lumpur, 1984

——— *Labour and Manpower Report 1981/82* Ministry of Labour, Kuala Lumpur, 1984

——— *Malaysia 1979 Official Year Book* Vol. 19, Kuala Lumpur: Government Printer, 1982

——— *Mid-Term Review, Fourth Malaysia Plan 1981–85* Kuala Lumpur: Government Printer, 1984

——— *Mid-Term Review, Second Malaysia Plan 1971–75* Kuala Lumpur: Government Printer, 1973

——— Ministry of Labour, Kuala Lumpur

——— *Money and Banking in Malaysia 1979* Bank Negara Malaysia, Kuala Lumpur, 1979

——— *Money and Banking in Malaysia 1980* Bank Negara Malaysia, Kuala Lumpur, 1980

——— *Money and Banking in Malaysia 1984* Bank Negara Malaysia, Kuala Lumpur, 1984

——— *Monthly Statistical Bulletin March, 1983* Department of Statistics, Kuala Lumpur, 1983

——— Public Works Department HQ, Road Section, Kuala Lumpur

——— Public Works Department HQ, Sabah, Kota Kinabalu

——— Public Works Department HQ, Sarawak, Kuching

——— *Sample Survey of Wholesale and Retail Trades in Peninsular Malaysia/Urban Area* Department of Statistics, Kuala Lumpur, various year

——— *Second Malaysia Plan 1971–75* Kuala Lumpur: Government Printer, 1971

——— *Survey of Distributive Trades* Department of Statistics, Kuala Lumpur, various years

——— Telecommunication Department, Kuala Lumpur, 1982

——— The Credit Guarantee Corporation (CGC), Bank Negara

——— Third Malaysia Plan 1976–80, Government Printers, Kuala Lumpur, 1976

——— *Timber Trade Review* 10, 4, Malaysian Timber Industry Board, Kuala Lumpur, 1981

——— Water Supply Division, Public Works Department, Kuala Lumpur

Means G.P. *Malaysian Politics* London: Hodder and Stoughton, 1976

Mohd. Suffian Hashim *An Introduction to the Constitution of Malaysia* Kuala Lumpur: Government Printer, 1972

Nasir L. 'A Study of Market Efficiency and Risk Return Relationship in the Malaysian Capital Market' Doctoral Dissertation, Katholieke Universiteit Leuven, 1983

Puthucheary J. *Ownership and Control of the Malaysian Economy* Singapore: Eastern Universities Press Ltd, 1960

Snodgrass D.R. *Inequality and Economic Development in Malaysia* Kuala Lumpur: Oxford University Press, 1980

Tan Koon Swan 'Public Enterprise: Restructuring and Chinese Capital Under the New Economic Policy' Paper presented at the Seventh Malaysian Economic Convention, Kuala Lumpur, 1983

Times National New Straits Times 20 October 1984

Tregouning K.G. *A History of Modern Malaya* London: Eastern Universities Press, 1964

Wang Gung Wu *Community and Nation: Essays on Southeast Asia and the Chinese* Kuala Lumpur: Heinemann, 1981

Winstedt R. *Malaya and its History* London: Hutchinson, 1966

World Bank *World Development Report 1980* New York: Oxford University Press, 1980

——— *World Development Report 1984* New York: Oxford University Press, 1984

Young K., Bussink W.C.F. and Hassan P. (eds) *Malaysia: Growth and Equity in a Multiracial Society* Baltimore: Johns Hopkins University Press, 1980

Index